Soul Fire

ACCESSING YOUR
Creativity

THOMAS RYAN

Walking Together, Finding the Way ®
SKYLIGHT PATHS ®
PUBLISHING
Woodstock, Vermont

Soul Fire: Accessing Your Creativity

2008 First Printing
© 2008 by Thomas Ryan

Grateful acknowledgment is given to reprint material from the following sources: Copyright Kripalu Center for Yoga & Health, all rights reserved. Originally published March 1, 2007, in the "Off the Mat" column of *Kripalu Online*, and titled "Living Life" by Laura Didyk.

Ryan, Thomas, Father.
Soul fire : accessing your creativity / Thomas Ryan.
p. cm.
Includes bibliographical references.
ISBN-13: 978-1-59473-243-0 (quality pbk.)
ISBN-10: 1-59473-243-4 (quality pbk.)
1. Spiritual life. 2. Creative ability—Religious aspects. 3. Creation (Literary, artistic, etc.)—Religious aspects. I. Title.
BL624.R865 2008
204'.4—dc22
2007048890

10 9 8 7 6 5 4 3 2 1

Manufactured in the United States of America
❀ Printed on recycled paper
Cover design: Jenny Buono

SkyLight Paths Publishing is creating a place where people of different spiritual traditions come together for challenge and inspiration, a place where we can help each other understand the mystery that lies at the heart of our existence.

SkyLight Paths sees both believers and seekers as a community that increasingly transcends traditional boundaries of religion and denomination—people wanting to learn from each other, walking together, finding the way.

SkyLight Paths, "Walking Together, Finding the Way," and colophon are trademarks of LongHill Partners, Inc., registered in the U.S. Patent and Trademark Office.

Walking Together, Finding the Way®
Published by SkyLight Paths Publishing
A Division of Longhill Partners, Inc.
Sunset Farm Offices, Route 4, P.O. Box 237
Woodstock, VT 05091
Tel: (802) 457-4000   Fax: (802) 457-4004
www.skylightpaths.com

To my sister,
Mary Jane,
who planted the seeds.

Contents

Introduction

Bellows and Coals

There are four things you should know about this book.

First, it certainly includes in its scope, but is by no means limited to, those "artistic types" who may already be proficient with color, sound, or verse. Creativity is something we *all* have, and there are myriad possibilities for the expression of our creative energies: cooking, gardening, painting, sculpture, carpentry, travel, dance, music, acting, sewing, writing, weaving, singing, and raising children, to name but some of them. *Soul Fire* is a way to help you find your medium and consciously cultivate it.

Second, while young adults could certainly draw inspiration from these pages, my target audience is those who are in the second half of their lives. What I share here was born out of my own experience of the growing urgency to attend to the creative fire that burns within. Whatever form the expression may take, the important thing is to be attentive to the smoldering ember within, smell the smoke, and fan the coals into flame. Failure to do so will leave a bed of cold ashes in the grate of the heart.

Third, *Soul Fire* is accessible to people of all faiths or none. I am a Christian and do not hesitate to draw from those wellsprings of inspiration. But, by the nature of my work, I also spend a significant amount of time engaged in interfaith encounters of various kinds, and that dimension of my life has been and continues to be an occasion for wonderful richness and blessing. I draw inspiration from other faith traditions as well as my own. As you'll see in the chapters that follow, those very encounters have stimulated my creativity.

Fourth, the medium is the message here. These pages contain both prose and poetry, with the latter exemplifying a primary vehicle of creative expression in this third phase of my life cycle. Both have their own feet and could stand alone. But I have woven the two together so that they might reinforce each other and communicate more holistically, speaking to both the right and the left sides of the brain, to our instrumental and affective capacities. Sometimes a poem, like a song or a painting, reaches a place in the heart where rational discourse never enters. More die for passion than for principles.

The medium is also the message inasmuch as the juxtaposition of prose and poetry represents the working together of those very polarities whose reconciliation is our life project—the rational and the intuitive, the masculine and the feminine.

My admittedly ambitious hope is, in symbolic terms, to strike a match with the prose and throw it on the dry kindling of your inner life as you read. And with the poetry, I hope to encourage you to find *your* creative expression, whatever that might be.

The place to start is with whoever you are and with the creative inclinations that mark your inner life. The questions for reflection and the exercises at the end of each chapter are designed to help you identify and cultivate these inclinations. The more time you give to engaging with them, the more you will get out of them.

The chapters move from a consideration of the urgency and potential of "the third birth" (after childbirth and adolescence, midlife) to a reflection on the nature of creativity, and then get down to practical things, such as map drawing, paths, and practices to cultivate your creativity—and the celebration of the spiritual gifts that come when you do.

These various angles of approach aim to serve you in accessing your creativity, in drawing warmth and vitality for your living from the fire that burns in your soul. I like to think of them as compressions of a bellows blowing upon the coals in the hearth of your heart, encouraging your struggling flame to rise up and dance.

Soul Fire

Throw open the door of that furnace
where the flames come leaping forth
like hungry hounds on the hunt,
licking and lapping at every cue on the trail
of the divine design for your life.
Ask not: where is it written?
It is written on your heart
in the colors of desire.
It is sung by the silent voices
of your recurring dreams.
It is the refrain chanted
by the chorus of your accumulating years:
"If not now, when? If not here, where?"
And the only obedience that will set you free
is surrender to the energy and fire
congealed in your gifts.

ONE

The Third Birth

THE URGENCY OF MIDLIFE

I remember the day: March 13, 1995. For the first time in eighteen years, I took up a pen to write a poem. And something within me stood, stretched its arms to the sky, and yelped like a kid emerging from the last day of class into the fresh air of summer.

As far back as grade school I can remember deriving enjoyment from rubbing words together and making something happen, like sparks from flint. I even gave up the freedom of the outdoors one summer in high school to take a poetry class offered as an elective. Numbers left me cold; it was words and ideas that lit my fire. Sophomore high school geometry was the last class I took that had anything to do with numeric equations. In college I carried a double major of English literature and philosophy, and my first job after college found me teaching writing and literature in California.

Then came graduate school in theology, with new demands on time and energy. The creative expression of poetry gave way to the more regimented format of footnoted term papers and thesis research. For almost the next two decades, vocational and professional development, with their related duties, left little psychic space for indulging poetic inspiration.

Then a fortuitous thing happened.

I joined my parents in Florida for a week in March. They had given themselves a treat of two winter months by the sea in their fiftieth anniversary year. It was an experiment they haven't repeated since, deciding in favor of their Minnesota winters in the "theater of the seasons." Though I love the invigorating days of the white landscape myself, I'm glad they tried Florida that year and invited me down because something important happened to me there.

Waiting for me at their place was one of my sister's care packages. My senior by two years, Mary Jane knows me well and occasionally will send me a surprise collection of things with which she feels I'd resonate. It's never brownies or pumpkin bread. That's not the kind of care package my sister sends. She considers me "fertile ground," and she specializes in "seeds."

When I opened the box I found a half-dozen audiotapes of talks given by the Welsh poet David Whyte, who now lives on the West Coast of the United States, where my sister had heard him speak. A note enclosed expressed how much these talks had spoken to her heart; she felt they would speak to mine as well.

This was one of those synchronistic events that Julia Cameron in *The Artist's Way* calls a "fortuitous intermeshing." I'd learned to trust my sister's instincts about these things, so I started listening.

"Life is inordinately fierce and difficult," were the words in my ear, "and no matter how you dress it up, this is always so." I could certainly relate to that!

Whyte went on to say that the word *bliss* comes from the French word *blessure* (or "wound") and suggested that bliss is the place in our lives where we are like a wound, open to the world. I came to a stop on the beach, turned the tape off, and sat down in the sand to listen to the dialogue going on within me.

At the time I was trying to hold down two full-time jobs. In one of them, I was rooted in the security of the "known," directing a national educational resource center for promoting Christian unity and interfaith understanding. In the other, I was in the process of "following my bliss," involved with founding a center for spirituality and meditation. But I didn't want to let go of the familiar and leap into the unknown in pursuit of this cherished dream until I could see that the new project was going to fly.

When I turned on the tape again, Whyte was reciting Robert Frost's poem "Fire and Ice":

> *Some say the world will end in fire,*
> *Some say in ice.*
> *From what I've tasted of desire*
> *I hold with those who favor fire.*

I was struck by Whyte's reflection that our life path is a tension between these two energy systems—fire and ice—and that there is no possibility of getting through without being singed or frozen at the edges. Then he recounted this traditional North American creation story:

Coyote steals fire and holds it close—too close, which is why he has brown fur. Raven then tries to steal the fire from Coyote and flies into the air, holding the fire in its beak. But Raven suffers a similar fate, which is why he has blackened feathers. When the fire falls to earth, Rattlesnake picks it up and holds it too close as well, and so got its distinct patterning down its back. In short, each creature got its unique markings from the way it was burned by fire.

Fire is a powerful element in most cultural and spiritual traditions. The Chinese consider fire one of the five basic forms of energy: water, earth, metal, wood, and fire. In Native American spirituality, the Eternal Fire is the center of the Medicine Wheel, which symbolizes the individual journey we each must take to find our own path. In Celtic mythology, fire is one of the elemental powers, and the lighting of the fire at Beltane marks a time of purification and transition. In Jewish and Christian scriptures, fire is often a symbol of holy presence, such as in the burning bush before Moses in the Hebrew Bible's Book of Exodus, and in the "tongues of fire" that appeared at Pentecost in the New Testament book of the Acts of the Apostles.

There is also a fire in the human soul. It burns like a lamp in a sanctuary too little visited. But for all that, it burns hot. And heat is energy.

With the passing of our years, the heat builds. And the energy, compressed and tightly contained, begins to whistle like a tea kettle on the stove. If there is anyone listening, the water will be poured out to make a drink—a potion, if you will—that restores and revitalizes. If not, the energy will be vaporized away—wasted—and the kettle rendered ineffective.

For three or four years I had been feeling these creative energies burning like a smoldering fire. I could feel the heat gathering within. I was forty-eight and aware that the time had come for me to be singed or frozen. I was feeling that particular midlife urgency to open up space for my creative energies. I suspected that there was a reservoir of creativity within me waiting to be tapped, wanting to be expressed, and I knew that I would have to choose fire to release it—even at the risk of getting singed. But I also knew that it was the only way to give fuller expression to something deep within.

At the midstage of life, the impatience of our inner reserve begins to make itself felt in various ways: the sense that we have brought to our present work all that we can and it is time for a new challenge; a vague but pervasive feeling of discontent with the configuration of activities and relationships in our life; a growing desire to step out and allow a recurring fantasy to become a reality.

However this inner pressure manifests itself, it is invariably accompanied by the realization that the image we have of ourselves is only a small reflection of our inner capacity. We become increasingly aware that there are rooms within us that have never been opened and explored, and the urgency to find the keys to open those doors increases as the sand in the hourglass becomes larger at the bottom than at the top.

Imperfect Connections

The desires of the human heart
fan out in myriad expressions.
The deepest one is often missed
and left to its digressions.

But when I try to wring from created
things the fullness of perfection,
I empty the sack of human lack
and find only imperfect connections.
Could it be that in the yearning
is the glory of this inner burning
vessel, whose deepest treasure lies
not in the satisfaction, but in the
desire that drives it until it dies?

THE STAKES ARE HIGH

I knew the risks. Undertaking a new work in midlife means a time of upheaval—of relationships, of routines based on familiarity, of one's inner equilibrium. If I left my work as director of the Canadian Center for Ecumenism, I would be stepping away from a ministry situation that was secure and satisfactory; away from twelve professional colleagues whose company I enjoyed; away from a work with all the helpful supports of library resources, international publication, high-tech equipment, and an endowment fund. With Unitas,* the fledgling spirituality and meditation center, I was stepping into a ministry situation where we had been given a magnificent mansion on a hill overlooking Montreal and the St. Lawrence River—but little else besides our own energy, faith, vision, and creativity.

I also knew that risk runs in both directions. When we are not true to our deepest, creative selves, we risk becoming dissatisfied with life, depressed. We may come to feel that nothing we do really matters or is worth the effort, and a dark cloud of meaninglessness can descend upon us. It is at this point that some begin to consume more alcohol or spend more and more time sitting in front of mindless entertainment on television. As the years roll on, some even come to hate themselves for wasting their time and talents, for not paying attention to the fire within.

In her book *The Second Half of Life*, cultural anthropologist Angeles Arrien describes the Four Rivers of Life—Inspiration, Challenge, Surprise, and Love—that support and sustain us and connect us to great gifts. The River of Inspiration reveals where we are in touch with our creative fire. The River of Challenge calls us to stretch and grow beyond what is knowable or familiar, to move past any fixed notion of what we can or can't do, to become explorers again. The River of Surprise keeps us fluid and flexible, inviting us to open to options and possibilities we had not considered, and to trust what emerges for our consideration. The River of Love shows where we are touched and moved by life's experience.

Many traditional societies believe that if we fail to stay connected to these rivers, we will succumb to "walking in the procession of the living dead" and begin to experience the soul loss, depression, and stagnation that are the manifestations of what the Eastern Christian spiritual fathers called *acedia*—a Greek word meaning "not caring"—and what Thomas Aquinas defined as "the lack of energy to look at new things."

---

*The story of the early years of Unitas (Latin for "unity") is related in fuller account in my book *Four Steps to Spiritual Freedom* (Mahwah, NJ: Paulist Press, 2003).

Carl Jung, one of the founders of modern psychology, believed that the second half of life was the crucial time to recognize, take ownership of, and express our creative energies that in younger days have been sentenced to "the dungeons of our subconscious" by the ruling authorities of career and/or family development. He saw this claiming of our creativity not just as a matter of whether we might eventually get to indulge a few of our hobby inclinations, but as a significant issue for our spiritual lives.

As Peter O'Connor relates in his book *Understanding Jung, Understanding Yourself*, in the first half of our lives we develop a public persona through which we interact with the outer world. We may have worked hard to build a strong identity through the pursuit of a career and a particular vocational status, be it in marriage and family life or in remaining single. In the second half of our lives, however, we are in a position to allow other dimensions of ourselves to emerge from the shadows—gifts and abilities that, up until now, have been marginalized because of the demands of other life tasks on our energies.

We are usually much more familiar with our outer, quantitative life experiences: birthdays, weddings and anniversaries, graduations and bar/bat mitzvahs, job opportunities, accidents and physical injuries, relationship breakups, funerals, championship games, travel adventures. The more internal, qualitative experiences—subtle, numinous, mystical—are generally less familiar to us. We might experience them as inner stirrings or disturbances that provoke insights, dreams, breakthroughs, or unexpected glimpses of the mysterious aspects of who we are.

The second half of our lives presents us with the opportunity to allow these other areas of our personalities to emerge and be accepted as part of who we are, to integrate them into what Jung called the Self. Think of the Self as the sun of the psychic solar system. Like a magnet, it draws all the separate parts of the psyche and unites the personality, giving us a sense of standing on solid ground.

For most people, this process does not seem to get going in earnest until the second half of life. In fact, it is often most pronounced in successful individuals who, at the midpoint of their lives, start experiencing difficulties. This integration of our outer and inner selves often takes the form of confrontation, which we have come to refer to—jokingly, but often accurately—as a "midlife crisis." Trying to embrace our interests and abilities that never got tapped and, at the same time, holding onto the other part of us—the life of details, the career responsibilities, and the duties of motherhood/fatherhood or service—can produce some serious tension.

In truth, this confrontation may be necessary because our outer self, our persona before the world, has labored hard to build an empire and will not easily relinquish control. The negotiating of this new image of ourselves, similar to childbirth with its contractions and to adolescence with its tumultuous passage through puberty, is sometimes called the "third birth" and is not without its own turmoil. As our inner world becomes more and more real, the discrepancy between our inner and outer lives becomes more pronounced and demands redress.

This tension is key: out of the collision of opposing forces, the sparks of creativity are generated. The integration of all the diverse parts of ourselves catalyzes a release of creative energy and becomes the critical process of growth in the second half of life.

If we don't grow—if we do not bridge the separation between our inner and outer worlds—we end up denying whole areas of our human experience. Jung saw this separation as dangerous for the health and well-being of the whole person. There is no wholeness, he believed, without a recognition and integration of the opposites within. Without balance in our lives, we become lopsided or incomplete. Rather than choosing one world over the other, we need to become adept at living in both.

Whether or not we engage in this inner work of integration is a matter of some consequence. The stakes are high in coming to grips with the fact that we are much more than the public persona that we have so painstakingly constructed in the first half of our lives. During the second half, we have the opportunity to meaningfully integrate who we have been, who we are, and who we can be.

Two Rivers

Two rivers,
each following its course for years,
their waters carrying cargo from
different ports of call,
now greet one another
and mix their currents,
flowing strongly forward as one.

At sunset through the trees along the banks,
light turns silver on the water,
and holds me in hypnotic trance,
revealing my life in the swift-running current.
Though rocks protrude and fallen trees obstruct,
the river flows on, moving in response
to some invisible call.

Am I really feeling or only dreaming
that this energy coursing through me
hears its echo in the water
tumbling over rocks?
No dam will hold for long;
all must surrender to this eternal flow
and find its fulfillment in the sea.

RECONNECTING WITH CREATIVE ENERGY

The human drive to connect with and give expression to our dormant creative energies transcends culture, race, and religion, though we are shaped by all of them. Hindus, for example, recognize four stages in the life cycle: the student (a time for learning), the householder (applying this education through marriage and child-rearing), the "forest dweller" (a time to step away and reflect on what we have experienced), and the sage (pursuing a state of freedom from desire).

Other cultures have similar understandings of human development. The Chinese, for example, have a saying: "In office a Confucian; in retirement, a Taoist." As we age, the "Confucian" mentality, concerned with practicalities, slowly yields to the "Taoist" mentality of contemplating nature's ways and nourishing our poetic spirit. This corresponds to Jung's view that, in the second half of life, we tend to grow more reflective and try to accept what our life has amounted to thus far. This is much akin to the last two of psychologist Erik Erikson's eight stages of human development: generativity versus stagnation, and integrity versus despair.

The way these stages of the life cycle are framed and named may vary with the cultural and religious context, but the underlying substructure of the process is the same: We learn. We apply. We step back and reflect. We savor.

During my holiday in Florida with my parents, I was just entering the "step back and reflect" stage. One afternoon I walked down to the beach and saw them sitting side by side in the sand. I stopped and took a long, loving look at them, riding the tide of emotion within my chest. That surge of feeling stirred something in me, and I felt a flash of poetic impulse. I had thought my poetry-writing days were long gone, but perhaps I hadn't recognized the creative impulse or I hadn't made time to give it expression. I had fallen, instead, into the prose-habit, writing books, articles for magazines, newspaper columns, homilies.

Later that afternoon I wrote my first poem in eighteen years:

Golden Anniversary

I saw them from a distance
sitting in their beach chairs side by side.
He, with his head tilted slightly back,
eyes closed as if intently listening
to the hiss and rumble of waves.
She, watching two pelicans skim the water,
her now-white head turning as they passed,
close-cropped curls bobbing in the breeze.
The people strolling by provided all
they longed to read, the gulls and breakers
their symphony of sound.

Are these the ones I've known
whose lives were filled with harvest moons
and kitchen chores?
His hand caressed the sand like kitten's fur,
senses full of winter sun's soft kiss
and the sea choir's chant.
Together they sat, side by side,
seeking nothing more than to be
in their peaceful communion
born of fifty years.

When my mom and dad took me to the airport, I felt that inner surge again as I looked out from the plane window and saw them behind the glass in the observation area. I reached for a magazine in the seat pocket in front of me and caught the emotional charge in another poem, scribbled out on the back cover:

View from a Runway

From where I sat below the propeller
his white cap and her snowy head shown
through the observation room's tinted glass.
Too many flights ago to recall,
a silent ritual of farewell
took shape by their mutual assent.
They do not turn and leave until
the plane's silver glint merges with cloud
and bids the heart to release its grasp.
They did not want for other things to do,
but in their silent vigil behind the tinted glass
we knew we mattered most.

Those days at the beach were the beginning of my reconnection with my creative energies. I took the little risk of self-expression in a way that felt new because it had been sidelined for so long. There is something enlivening about expanding our self-definition, and a risk does exactly that. Each poem I wrote became the ground for future efforts. I continue to work at opening up space in my life for these creative impulses—as the poetry in this book testifies—and I am becoming reconciled with a part of myself that had been relegated to "the shadow."

EMBRACING THE SHADOW

My brother Michael carries high the banner of my family's Irish heritage. He enjoys nothing more than an evening out listening to music in an Irish pub and sipping a Guinness. He even flies the Irish flag from his home. Once, while on a business trip to Chicago, he flew back to Minneapolis in the evening to hear three Irish tenors sing in concert and then returned to Chicago the next morning.

Michael's outer persona is a civil trial lawyer. It's a persona that is well established, and he is successful in his career. He served as Minnesota's state representative to DRI—*The Voice of the Defense Bar*, a national organization of lawyers who specialize in the defense of civil lawsuits—and his colleagues honored him nationally with the State Representative of the Year Award in 2006. He has also been named a "Super Lawyer" by a local legal publication.

But this "super lawyer" has a recurring fantasy: to open his own authentic Irish pub where he can talk and laugh and share the ups and downs of life day and night with patrons. Jung had a term for that place in our psyche where we harbor our unfulfilled fantasies: the "shadow." It denotes the part of our personality that we repress or don't talk much about because it is not in accord with the way we either are allowed to be (by professional profile, by family, by teachers) or wish to perceive ourselves. If our fantasy does not fit in with our profession as, say, a trial lawyer, then it gets relegated to the shadow, where it survives on the crumbs that fall from the table.

Though many think of the "shadow side" as something negative—something that contradicts the goals and values we consciously hold—Jung also spoke about the "shadow" as a potential source of richness. As long as it is hidden, it is unavailable to us, but when it becomes conscious, there is a treasure trove of energy released. We can put our "shadow" aspirations on hold for only so long before the pressure from within begins to make itself felt in our lives. The more we recognize and accept these buried instincts and desires, the more fully we can live.

Today my brother Michael has found a way of expressing his inner fantasy. In addition to periodic pub visits for a music fix (where he sometimes takes the stage as a drummer), he belongs to a gourmet club, a group of friends with whom he and his wife enjoy good food, socialize, and travel. They recently returned from a group trip to—you guessed it—Ireland!

My sister, Mary Jane, has also found a way to tap into her shadow side. She had always been the "brain" in the family, setting a high academic standard for the four of us boys who followed. She was at the top of her high school honor roll and brought home numerous trophies in speech and debate. Her favorite reading was *U.S. News and World Report*. As for me and my brothers, the "geometry" of sports—the football gridiron, the baseball diamond, the basketball court, and the oval of the running track—had a lock on our primary energies. It hardly seemed fair: we did not escape her influence, but she escaped ours. She seemed destined to live her life as one of those people who would never do anything more physically challenging than take a walk.

Then she and her husband came to participate in one of my meditation and yoga retreats at Unitas. For the first time since her playground life in grade school, she connected with her body and felt at home in it. Much to my surprise, she and her husband maintained their yoga practice back home throughout the year and returned for an advanced retreat the following summer.

As Mary Jane tapped into this whole new dimension of herself, she was amazed at the energy released in her life. To my delight and astonishment, she enrolled in a yoga teacher-training certification program, got a job at a local yoga center, and is now teaching yoga on weekends.

By the third time she came to Unitas, she had a whole new lease on life. She had dropped the bucket into a deep well of energy inside her and could not get enough of its regenerative powers.

Transitions

Leaf fall, snow fall;
　　growth that looks like loss.
Green buds, bark shards, begonias;

growth that looks like gain.
Seasonal sleight of hand.

Call its bluff—rake the garden leaves
   for new growth.
There is more than
   death and endings here.

And in the fallow season
   when things go slowly
or nothing seems to change,
   faith is formed from the world
of feather and foliage.

Suddenly
   the eggshell cracks
      the branch blossoms
         the bird molts

And the end
   becomes a new
      beginning.

THE SECRET TO STAYING FULLY ALIVE

By some happy alchemy, I had triggered a process of awakening in my sister's life, and with her "seed" package of David Whyte tapes, she had catalyzed a release of creative energy in mine. I don't think it was an "accident" that these events happened to us in the second half of life.

The dissatisfaction and discontent so often associated with midlife is the very call to explore that fertile valley within where so many underground springs are waiting to be discovered and to be put on the map of Who We Are. It is the call to explore the terrain of our personality more comprehensively and to recover our lost treasure of creativity. Or, as Jung would put it, it is our call to individuation, to wholeness, to be in harmony with the whole world—without and within.

This is the secret to staying energized and thoroughly alive: staying attuned to the creative spirit within and allowing it expression. Many studies have confirmed that cultivating our creativity in the second half of life strengthens our morale, contributes to physical health as we age, enriches relationships, and is, in the end, our greatest legacy.

When we are children, our creative energies romp within us like puppies in the yard. But when we grow up, they bark like dogs in a kennel—leaping and yapping to be uncollared, to be let out to run in the beckoning sunlight and open fields or flat expanses of beach. But if this is to happen, something has to give—the equivalent of a leash, a collar, a locked gate. Something has to shift to make way—an agenda book, a routine of evenings spent staring passively at the tube, an image of ourselves and of what we are capable.

Listen to the way Laura Didyk, an editor and writer for the Kripalu Center for Yoga and Health in Stockbridge, Massachusetts, describes her experience of the gate opening. For her, it happened while watching a live concert clip of R&B singer John Legend:

> John Legend comes out on a stage, opens his mouth, spreads his arms to his fans, and gives himself over to this thing that is his. "Here I am," he is saying, like the singing itself is his way of saying "thank you" to whatever beautiful and intelligent force gave him this gift. I cry because I've wasted a lot of time trying to batten down the hatches of my spirit, to shush all the stuff clanking around inside that is dying to get out.

Over the years, I've managed to build an intricate shell around my longing, around the undeniable urge to create and express. This shell has kept me quieter than I really am, less funny, less animated, and more afraid. But the shell is beginning to crack. Sometimes, the fissure produces just a fine dusting, but it gets me one thin, microscopic layer closer to the core. Other times, a palm-sized shard will fall to the ground in one satisfying shatter. Even half-revealed, my spirit is brighter and more alive. Watching John Legend on stage, shining his light for all to see, makes me want the fully expressed life so much that it hurts.

Some people can live their whole lives with a gnawing feeling in their stomachs that there are things they want to do, if only they were braver; demons they should face, if only they thought they could survive it; a connection to something bigger than themselves, if only they were worth it; a much brighter, fuller, richer life they could be living if things were, well, different. I was one of those people, waiting for my life to magically take shape on its own....

Whatever I was waiting for so I could live the life I thought I was meant to live, wasn't coming.... So I made a decision. I decided that the lives I saw other people living, other people succeeding at, could maybe one day be mine. I decided that if I didn't take some action on my own behalf, I wasn't going to be able to live with myself.... My fear of not becoming who I knew I was meant to be loomed larger than my fear of failing or suffering or looking stupid....

I started to spend time with people—friends, spiritual teachers, artists, writers—whose inner lives attracted me. I immersed myself in literature, music, film, whatever I could find that made me want to keep going, to live better and louder and with more color and verve. I ventured out to see live music, plays, dance performances. I attended poetry readings. I took walks....

I don't know at what moment or on what day it arrived—this presence, right below my heart, a feeling I've come to recognize as strength—I just know it's there now. When it wanes, I remember myself at twelve years old, powering my body full speed into a round-off back handspring then up into the dreamy float of a lay-out flip. I remember what true, unbridled determination feels like, and find the strength again to allow the universe to carry me deeper and deeper into the center of my beautiful, sensational, fabulous, illuminated life.

Laura's story wonderfully captures the essence of this book: becoming ever more fully alive, ever more our creative selves. She is now a published essayist, poet, and fiction writer enjoying her "illuminated life."

An Awareness That

It might come upon you as you step from the lake
and see the striped back of a water moccasin
slither off the rocks and through the lily pads

or maybe you will recognize it on a forest hike
in the apprehensive way your eyes dart about for bears
your mind constantly rehearsing what will I do if...

but come it will in what is wild and free:
the awareness that these woods or this lake
do not particularly care if you live or die

the awareness of how the seemingly solid bottom
of your life can drop out from under you like a trap door
suddenly leaving your five-year plan in free fall

the awareness that the more exalting experiences
that expand the heart and make the spirit dance
only come with a consciously calculated measure of risk.

QUESTIONS FOR REFLECTION

Where would you locate yourself in these four phases of the life cycle?

> We learn.

> We apply.

> We step back and reflect.

> We savor.

If the path through life is a tension between two energy systems—fire and ice—and there is no possibility of getting through without being singed or frozen at the edges, which of these two images speaks most to your present life situation?

Do you relate to any of these lines?

> A sense that you have brought to your present work all that you can and it is time for a new challenge.

> A vague but pervasive feeling of discontent with the configuration of activities and relationships in your life.

> A growing desire to step out and allow a recurring fantasy to become a reality.

What are some of your interests and abilities that seldom get tapped?

Think back to your years in grade school or junior high. Do you remember having any areas of instinctive natural interest that, as you moved on into high school, you were not allowed to develop or indulge? Rummage around a bit in your "shadow side" to see what undeveloped interests may still be lurking there after all these years.

David Whyte says that when we lose faith in our own voice, or have no faith that our inner and outer worlds can meet, we are like one hand clapping. But "when the inner and outer worlds do meet like two hands clapping, you get a sharp, clear sound. This is your soul, your poem, your voice." What experiences can you point to in your life when your inner and outer worlds met and there was a "sharp, clear sound" that expressed the fire in your soul?

EXERCISES TO ACCESS YOUR CREATIVITY

Find a photo of yourself showing a time when you were happy, carefree and/or content. Post it in a place where you see it each morning. Think about what conditions contributed to these feelings. How could you recreate one of these conditions *today*?

Write down some projects or interests or travel destinations that, along the way, you have put "on hold" until you had more time or money. Take some time to look at your list. Ask yourself whether you could possibly undertake any of them now.

Imagine that you are eighty years old. Look back on your life and list the things you will have regretted not having done. Choose one of the items on your list and map a plan of five to ten steps that could lead to accomplishing that goal. What's the first thing you can do this week to work toward that goal?

The Rendezvous

One's deepest self is like a timid fawn
that stays among the forest ferns
and only ventures forth at dawn.
One must patiently wait, with outstretched hand,
waiting for the feathered one to land.
One must create the sacred space
and order quests of lesser note
to be faithful to the time and place.
Then, constant to the rendezvous,
sit still and clear as morning dew
and your true self will be revealed to you.

TWO

The Nature of Creativity

WE ALL HAVE IT

In concrete terms, creativity is the ability to see new possibilities in set ways of doing things, whether it relates to making a meal or arranging the furniture in a room, designing cars or opening a business. It is the capacity of interpreting old stories, music, and dance forms in new ways. It is taking the nearest exit out of the traffic jam on the highway and getting there by the back roads. It's using a paper clip or bobby pin to hold the machine together long enough to finish the job. It's a salesman putting the right words together to get in the door, or a surgeon responding on the spot to an unanticipated problem.

Creativity. We all have it and we all use it. The mother dancing among the needs of three children. The coach keeping the volatile mix of personalities on his roster playing as a team. The teacher bringing the slowest and the fastest along together. Creativity is not a gated square into which only professional artists and writers and dancers are allowed to enter, but a public park through which all pass. Each morning when we put our feet on the floor, we are facing a fresh canvas. What brush, what colors will we use to create something interesting and attractive on this virgin space before us?

Creativity is not an "extra" but a necessity for living. As the familiar proverb credited to Plato states, "Necessity is the mother of invention." Creativity is a fundamental part of our uniqueness. We are each made in the image and likeness of the Creator and, at the very least, that means that we, too, are endowed with creativity.

> Humans ... create stories and songs, pictures and sculptures, rockets that fly to the moon and beyond, machines and medicines that help heal the human body and mind, networks of instant communication and information that link the diverse peoples of the whole planet. Humans create new forms of society and economy and ways of being and living on the earth. We have free will, the power to create our destiny, the very pattern and course of our lives. Such godlike powers are not dispensed to just a few geniuses and seers, but *to all of us* [italics added for emphasis].
> —DAN WAKEFIELD, *Releasing the Creative Spirit*

We are all born originals. The unfortunate thing is that, along the way, so many of us become copies. We let others do our thinking for us and chart our route.

Think back to when you were growing up and going through school. How many kids—maybe yourself?—were put into a "science track" and then sat in math and chemistry and physics classes while their natural inclinations toward shop or art class or band got shelved or abandoned? How many times were you told to stop daydreaming and pay attention? Or lectured on the need to get all your homework done before you could play? Or admonished, "That's fine for a hobby, but what are you going to do to earn a living?"

Sadly, we live in a culture that has little time for what cannot be easily pictured or managed. Our Western culture's focus on being productive, on gaining more, on being "the best" allows little room for the sometimes messy and inefficient process of creativity. In America's profile before the world, it is the practical and empirical that dominates. But if we are the scientific and organizational leaders of the world, we are also its cultural adolescents. How else can we explain that art and poetry are, as one editor shared, "the two bottom rungs of the publishing ladder in this country"?

From a pragmatist's perspective, poetry is almost without utility, an indulgence in fancy, a pretty packaging of idea and sentiment. Given the roadblocks along the way, it's not surprising that many people simply pack up their poetic impulses and put them aside, leaving the "creating" to someone else. For some, the denial of creativity is just a habit: "Oh, I've never done anything like that. I wouldn't know where to begin." For others, it's fear: "Who me, I'm not creative! I don't have [the skill, the talent, the patience, the training—whatever!] for that. I'm just an ordinary sort of person." And for others, it's busyness: "Oh, I used to dabble in painting [or writing stories or drawing "dream house" plans], but who has time for that now?"

If the first key to accessing our creativity is to recognize that we are made in the image of the Creator—with the capacity to create—then surely the second key is to give ourselves permission—even an invitation—to create!

When a music teacher tells students who are learning new instruments, "If you're going to make a mistake, make it loud!" the teacher is saying, in effect, "You have permission to make mistakes—so relax and enjoy the process." Or when a drama teacher says to those who have forgotten their lines, "Improvise!" she is affirming that they have the creativity within themselves to keep things moving, so tap into it. The permission from without supports the permission from within. Soon the actors, the musicians, are less afraid of flubbing and are having more fun. Their creativity is encouraged by trial and error rather than dampened by inner criticism.

Some projects "cry out for a pencil," and we need to give ourselves permission to scribble outside of the lines:

The Quality of Lead

Some projects cry out for a pencil.
They know they're not ready for nails or cement
because there's no blueprint or stencil.
They need scrap paper, wastebaskets,
time to think, before they're ready to take shape
in the dark and decisive character of ink.
They know that creativity is shot dead
when there's no room to scribble with
that soft, erasable, fine-pointed lead.

TRANSFORMATION OF THE ORDINARY

Experiments in neuroscience have demonstrated that we arrive at the way we understand the world in roughly this sequence: First, our senses bring us selective information about what is out there. Second, the brain constructs its own simulation of the sensations. Third, only then do we have our first conscious experience of our surroundings.

In other words, the world comes into our consciousness as a construction of our own making, filtered through our senses and our brains. We may *think* we see and hear everything that is out there, but when we remember that owls see in the dark and dogs hear sounds above our range of hearing, we recognize that our human senses are selective. We perceive only the sensations we are programmed to receive for our survival, and we recognize only those for which we have mental maps. In short, we see and hear only a fraction of what is possible.

Creativity asks us, in the midst of the contrarieties of daily living, to believe there are new possibilities out there, to loosen our control and take more risks, to let life unfold. The creative process in general—and art in particular—is about rearranging *us*, opening us up emotionally, exposing us to surprising presences, and coming up with new combinations of possibilities.

In her book *A Return to Love*, Marianne Williamson invites us to listen to the deep intuitions within and to see ourselves in terms of these possibilities:

> Our deepest fear is not that we are inadequate. Our deepest fear is that we are powerful beyond measure. It is our light, not our darkness, that most frightens us. We ask ourselves, Who am I to be brilliant, gorgeous, talented, fabulous? Actually, who are you not to be? You are a child of God. Your playing small does not serve the world. There is nothing enlightened about shrinking so that other people won't feel insecure around you. We are all meant to shine, as children do. We were born to make manifest the glory of God that is within us. It's not just in some of us; it's in everyone. And as we let our own light shine, we unconsciously give other people permission to do the same. As we are liberated from our own fear, our presence automatically liberates others.

Artist Gertrud Mueller Nelson tells a wonderful story in *To Dance with God* about a sixteen-year-old girl named Annika, whose creativity liberated her mother's as well. Annika had just discovered a creative outlet for herself in printing on fabric. One day, her mother interrupted Annika's printing to send her on an errand. A guest was coming and Annika's mother had forgotten to pick up some asparagus. So Annika put aside the printing blocks she had carved out of erasers and potatoes, washed off her paint smudges, and hurried to the market down the hill. When she came back, she slid the brown bag across the counter to her mother and said with delight, "Just look at what *else* I bought."

She let her mother fish in the bag, pulling out first the asparagus and then a fat yam.

"But we don't need this. It doesn't go with the menu. Whatever did you think we could do with a single yam?" said the mother, carrying on about the absurdity of the purchase and its impracticality.

But her daughter stood firm. "No," she insisted, "just *look* at it. Have you ever seen such a fine, fat root? It's beautiful. I bought it for me, to make a large print with. My erasers and those little potatoes are so small. Besides, it's just too lovely."

And with that she proceeded to slice it open, exclaiming about the color inside and urging her mother to look as it lay split and golden-orange on the cutting board.

"We both saw it," her mother said. "A wonderful yam, a perfectly glorious fat, firm root." And then she reflected how the artist in herself saw the emerging artist in her daughter, and she understood all over again that being awake to new possibilities is the realm of the artist in all of us. The ordinary that we had not even noticed becomes wonderful. "The vision that we long for," she said, "lies just the other side of the practical. In that dusty root, the humdrum and the fabulous are joined."

All it takes to transform the ordinary into the extraordinary is a long, loving look at the real. It's the art of contemplative looking and listening with the eyes and ears of both head and heart. Creativity is not something magical or mystical. It is a matter of looking at quotidian realities, such as yams—or clouds—and seeing something extraordinary in them.

Clouds

> My calling is carried in the clouds
>> born in water
>> enspirited by wind
>> drawn and sent by the sun
>> transfigured by light

A way of life is passing overhead
  free as grace they move across the earth
    looking as soft and gentle as combed cotton
    yet carrying fearsome power in their folds
    changing form to fit the hours
    revealing gold in rainbow showers

My story is written in the clouds
  always changing on the surface
  but of stable elements composed
  just like those in the realm of glory
  even when they pass and disappear
  they're acting on our atmosphere

LIFE ITSELF IS A CREATIVE ACT

In her poem "God's World," Edna St. Vincent Millay captures a hint of what it takes to make the human journey creative:

Long have I known a glory in it all,
  But never knew I this;
  Here such a passion is
As stretcheth me apart ...

There is a lot to be said for being "stretched apart." Any time we can stretch ourselves beyond the familiar—make forays beyond the familiar into surprising places, unexpected experiences, unfamiliar cultures—we not only have an opportunity to learn new things and gain stimulating insights but also the chance to see how creative the act of living really is.

In 1991 I was able to make one such foray. For three months I plunged myself into the kaleidoscopic interreligious world of India on a study sabbatical. It was a time in which the unfamiliar vastly outweighed the familiar on a daily basis. It was not an easy and comfortable time on any level—psychological, intellectual, spiritual, or physical. The harvest of learning and insight, however, was well worth the cost in human terms. It was a quarter that gave me new life, vision, and energy. It was the place where I began to appreciate that the sheer negotiation of life itself from one end of the day to the other is a creative act.

India does not leave anyone indifferent. If you have been born and raised in North America, nothing really prepares you for the experience of India. If you go beyond the five-star hotels, the "safe" restaurants, and first-class travel, India will assault your senses and turn all your conventional understandings of how things should work upside down and inside out. A single travel experience (by no means exceptional) from my trip captures the essence of the creative means by which people literally make their way.

One day, while trying to find transport from the Hindu holy city of Rishikesh (named after the *rishis*, or sages) to Dharamsala, the Dalai Lama's Buddhist colony in the Himalayas, I backpacked to the auto rickshaw stand about a mile away. The rickshaw is a three-seater, built to take two in the front seat along with the driver, three in the middle, and three in the back. We were four in the front, four in the middle, and five in the back. When we arrived at the bus stand, people were in a state of panic. It was New Year's in the Hindu calendar, and everyone was trying to get on a bus to get home. People were crawling in and out of the windows, climbing on top of the bus.

I jammed myself in with my backpack for a forty-five-minute ride from Rishikesh to Haridwar, where I was going to try to catch a night train. The bus was full but more people kept fighting their way on, until the aisle had twenty people standing cheek-to-jowl, grabbing for anything to steady themselves as the bus lurched out. Others were running alongside the bus, shoving their bags through broken windows, and catching the arms of friends who pulled them in.

In Haridwar I took a bicycle rickshaw to the train station. The city streets here, too, were in a festival mood. At the train station I learned that the only train for Pathenkot, which would take me to Dharamsala, had left over two hours ago. An hour later, and my fourth time back up to the "Inquiries" window, I was told that if I caught a bus to Roorkee, a forty-five-minute trip, I could still catch the train—which had now left over *three* hours ago. I decided not to waste time trying to figure out the logic of that, and I headed for the bus station.

The bus station was pandemonium. Buses were arriving every few minutes into a big gravel parking lot, with no signs saying where they were coming from or where they were going. Each time a bus arrived, a crowd surged around it, demanding to know where this bus was destined. Some struggled off, others on.

An hour later I finally worked my way onto a bus going through Roorkee. It was a "capacity 40," according to the sign over the driver, but I counted eighty-three heads on the bus—and I couldn't see all of them! I was standing up behind the driver, straddling the antiquated gear box, hanging on to the back of the driver's seat for balance. Between my legs I could see a man's big sack and two feet, and I realized that my rear end was in his face. Every time the driver shifted, I searched for space on the floor to move my feet to accommodate the action. Once out of town, we stopped along the road and everyone on the bus emptied onto the shoulder of the road. It was the only way the ticket seller could get money from people for the trip; there was no room on the bus for him to move down the aisle.

On the road again every minute was ripe for narrow misses with oxcarts, cyclists whose loads were wide with produce, cows meandering across the road, and other buses and trucks. There was just one narrow, twelve-foot-wide strip of asphalt, and everybody moving in both directions—by foot, bicycle, moped, car, truck, oxcart, tractor, and bus—seemed to claim it. The horn was the bus driver's response to everything that moved into his field of vision.

Finally we creaked into Roorkee and the bus squeezed me out. As I turned back to look at it, with my feet gratefully on terra firma, I could see that there were at least thirty people in the luggage rack on top, hanging on for dear life.

Welcome to India, where a simple bus trip between point A and point B is a creative act.

Creativity can take so many expressions! When a computer programmer designs a new program, when the roller-blader dances on wheels, when the chiropractor exerts just the right maneuver to realign the hips, when the investor sells his stock at the opportune time—all are letting their "own light shine," to use Marianne Williamson's phrase. Each effort is an art, a creative mélange of training, inspiration, and savoir-faire much like a dancer's choreography, a singer's aria, or a poet's turn of phrase.

Nothing is too "ordinary" to be creative. When people do what they do well, they are turning the ordinary into art, making an art of living. Perhaps you remember the national collegiate football championship in January 2003 between Ohio State and Miami. It was described as possibly the best bowl game in history. Decided on the last play of the second overtime, it was a knuckle-cracking, make-your-voice-hoarse standoff between two sets of savvy coaches and heroic athletes. It was state-of-the-art football. Brilliant conception and brilliant execution. I don't know about you, but I went to bed that night energized and inspired.

In much the same way, "state-of-the art" living requires a similar passion. It has nothing to do with high-end technology or luxury accommodations. The art of living is a matter of seeing our lives as our own creation and ourselves as producers and directors of it. It is a matter of embracing life with passion and energy, of doing what we do well. When we can welcome the "glory in it all," as Edna St. Vincent Millay would say, our lives can go from black-and-white to Technicolor, from routine to art. We are participating in the greatest artistic creation of all—life!

Creativity

Sometimes it feels like crawling into the brush
   after a dangerous thing, foolhardy and naïve,
      like those two campers I took once
      on a hike into a river canyon
      who sighted a rattler sidewinding into the bushes
         and went in after it
         pulling it out by the tail.

Did they see the fear in my face
   when one held it up to me
   with a firm grip behind the head
   jaws gaping and tail writhing
   in the shimmering August heat?

Pulling a tiger or any dangerous thing by the tail
from its hiding place is as unsettling as creativity
and has fierce consequences.

At other times it gently rises up within,
soft as sleep, all unordered and unsought,
like bubbles rising up from the bottom of a lake
or a spontaneous stretch in bed overtaking you
somewhere between awakening and arising.

All of a sudden you become aware
that there is an energy moving you,
  silently lifting upward
      from the bottom of your being
          like a hot-air balloon slowly taking flight
and you know you have no choice
but to let yourself be carried
on the currents of the wind.

Or had you something more predictable in mind
  than this unexpected little ride?

QUESTIONS FOR REFLECTION

Think back to when you were in grade school. What interested you then? What seemed to come naturally to you? What has happened to those inclinations and talents over the years?

In what areas of your life do you feel "frozen"? What are some things you could do to begin to give yourself permission to "scribble," to experiment with something different?

Think of the events of your life that comprise a typical week. Can you see ways in which getting from your "point A to point B" is a creative act?

What things do you do well? How do these things reflect your innate creativity?

EXERCISES TO ACCESS YOUR CREATIVITY

Notice the eye color of everyone with whom you come in contact today.

Listen to a different radio station today, one you've never listened to before.

Get up ten to twenty minutes earlier tomorrow and take a different route to work/school/the store.

Wedding Feast

My life is a wedding feast,
a crescendoing celebration
of the slow-growing union
of two in love. I know now
that when all present could see
the shortfall, it was you
who filled my empty jar
with living water, just as
it is you who are changing
each day's living into wine.

THREE

Your Creative Journey

A CREATIVE JOURNEY ROAD MAP

When I talk to people about making a "road map" of their creative journey, I'm talking about charting how particular events in their lives have opened them to wonder, cultivated their curiosity, and given them new ideas.

"What unleashed new emotions in you?" I ask them. "When, where, how have you been inspired to consider new possibilities? What changed the angle of your living, brought you into the presence of the Holy, and made you aware of the restless yearning of your heart for the ineffable?"

For each of us, making such a creative journey map starts with naming these specific experiences. I believe that this exercise is one of the key steps in recognizing the creativity already present in our lives— and accessing the latent creativity that is waiting to emerge. By seeking out the roots of our creative path, by identifying the experiences that have opened our minds and hearts and expanded our dreams, we tap into the very source of our creative growth.

Perhaps if I share some of the experiences on my creative journey map—experiences that captured my imagination and stretched it like the waistband of an undergarment that will never fit a narrower figure again—they will serve as a stimulus to your reflection. I can only briefly mention a few here, yet even in this abbreviated process of sharing my story, I become newly aware of how my life and ministry as an ecumenist—one who works for unity among Christians and understanding, respect, and mutual enrichment among followers of different religions—has nurtured my creativity and evoked admiration for other ways of living and praying. I can see ways that my creative development has given me a new appreciation for the presence and activity of the Creative Spirit in the world.

PERSONAL GLIMPSES

NEW FRONTIERS

*Experience: My first assignment as a campus chaplain,
Ohio State University, 1974*

As a new chaplain on campus, I decided to initiate a series of dialogue evenings by inviting students from the Lutheran, Wesleyan, Episcopal, United Church, and Hillel Centers to come to the Catholic Newman Center for an evening of sharing. The questions that guided our dialogue went something like this: What is important for us to know about you? What in your tradition do you love the most? What nourishes you? What would you like to know about us? Is there anything we could do together on campus? The point of the exercise was not agreement but to know and understand one another better.

Emboldened by the stimulating experience of these sharings, we decided to throw out a wider net. In subsequent series we hosted Quakers, Mennonites, Seventh-day Adventists, Latter-day Saints, and Jehovah's Witnesses. We were learning; misunderstandings were yielding to accurate information, and prejudices were crumbling.

As often happens when we are being creative and pushing new frontiers beyond our secure comfort zone, surprising outcomes stretch us even further. One day a phone call came inviting me to be the Catholic panelist on a weekly national televised program called *American Religious Town Hall Meeting*, sponsored by the Seventh-day Adventists. I did not feel up to this at all; I was just a "baby priest," and the oils of ordination were still wet on my hands. But there was a wizened old biblical scholar, Father Ed Peters, who, half-blind, lived in our Paulist community in Columbus. He encouraged me to accept, telling me, "I'll help you prepare."

And so it happened. I flew to Dallas, Texas, to tape six hour-long programs in which representatives of about eight denominations would sit at a round table and discuss a variety of topics.

I was being opened up to a wider world by leaps and bounds.

A TURNING POINT

Experience: Watching a young man direct traffic at Lake Lugano,
Italy, 1976

One summer during my three years of chaplaincy at Ohio State, two friends and I went on a backpacking trip through five countries in Europe. As I stood one evening at the entry point to the campground in Lake Lugano in northern Italy, watching the young man greet and direct the cars that arrived at the gate, I had a moment of awakening that changed the angle of my life. In observing this young man speak in German to cars arriving from Germany, in French to those arriving from France, in Spanish to those arriving from Spain, in English to those from England, I suddenly realized how much I had missed growing up in a monocultural, monolinguistic little town in southern Minnesota. Then and there I resolved to leap at the first chance that presented itself to live in another country and learn another language.

It didn't take long. Within the following year, there was an opening at the Newman Center at McGill University in Montreal, Canada. Because the Paulists are a North American community, there are only two opportunities available to live and work in the community outside the United States—in Canada and in Rome (where we staff the Church of Santa Susanna for ex-patriot Americans and all other English-speakers). Montreal, I figured, was as good as I was likely to get, and so I raised my hand.

Not only did I find myself director of a chaplaincy center in which the Presbyterian, United, Ukranian Orthodox, Christian Scientist, and Catholic campus ministers all had their offices on the same corridor, but also the bishop appointed me as a Catholic representative to the Montreal Council of Churches. It was through this network that I came to know and work with Father Irénée Beaubien, S.J., the founder-director of the Canadian Centre for Ecumenism.

Here's the thing about creativity: it's a living, growing, unpredictable entity. Once it emerges, you never know what course it will take. For me, that initial raising of my hand was already launching me in an unexpected direction. When the position of associate director came open at the Centre for Ecumenism, Father Beaubien invited me to apply, which I eventually did with the support of my community leadership.

A booster rocket was about to fire in my life and send me into another orbit, into worlds I had only heard or read about.

THE WORLD GETS BIGGER

Experience: Sitting in Canterbury Cathedral, England, 1980

In 1980–81 the Canadian Centre for Ecumenism sent me on a tailor-made sabbatical year that would provide me with not just book learning but also firsthand experience of living and studying with Anglican, Protestant, and Orthodox Christians in their historical matrix.

I began in England, spending a summer with Anglicans at the Canterbury Summer School and worshipping daily in the transporting space of Canterbury Cathedral. I never would have thought it possible to develop such affection for a structure of stone and glass. It was my first experience of the poetic spirit architecturally inscribed. I would sit in this historic church transfixed by the streams of light passing through the magnificent stained-glass windows. One day, as I sat looking at a window depicting Jesus washing the feet of his disciples, a little epiphany experience occurred. I saw that everything I was engaged in—the studies, the meetings, the discussions—was all ultimately about service. I saw that the essential vocation for people in all walks of life—married or single—is availability for service in love.

Stained-Glass Meditation

There you are again,
this time in reds and blues
—a stained-glass setting—
with your towel and basin
while Peter offers a reluctant foot,
his face covered in a cloud of consternation.

Halos on their heads now,
but not back then.
They still had to learn
as I do
that your way
is not our way.

This is the image
that schools me most:
the towel and the basin.
And you, on your knees
with your sleeves rolled up,
washing dirty feet.

AN APPRECIATION OF DIVERSITY

Experience: Five months at the Ecumenical Institute in Bogis-Bossey,
Switzerland, 1980–81

In the fall of my sabbatical year I became a member of an international community of fifty-five people from thirty-five different countries representing twenty-one different Christian denominations. We lived, studied, worked, and prayed together for five months at the World Council of Churches, Ecumenical Institute at Bossey, twelve miles outside of Geneva. The entire experience was an exercise in creativity, as we planned our own menus, worship services, and cultural evenings. The Africans and Asians were getting upset stomachs on Western-style foods. The Americans and Canadians in the group had to figure out how to present an entertaining evening of North American culture. (The Europeans told us—tongue in cheek, of course—that they were scheduling other activities for the second half of the evening because they were sure it would be a short program.) I was on the liturgy committee, searching for ways of worshipping together that would enable each of the community members to at least recognize a *little* something of their own tradition in the community's prayer life. And, of course, we were all learning from one another daily in class.

My vision of church was expanding like bread in the oven. I was learning to see the world and the church in fresh, new ways. I was being challenged to open up to other ways of doing things. I was becoming more flexible, more creative in searching for solutions to the problems we faced. I was becoming less rigid in my prayer forms and was relating to the Bible in new and life-giving ways. Perhaps most important of all, instead of being threatened by difference and diversity, I was learning to appreciate and celebrate it as a richness for the whole church.

LESSONS OF LIFE

Experience: A moment in traffic, Cairo, Egypt, 1981

In the spring of that sabbatical year, I took the plunge into the world of Eastern Christians in Egypt, Israel, Turkey, and Greece. It's remarkable how some of the most formative moments of our lives are not at formal conferences but come via things that people say or do naturally and spontaneously in the course of daily living.

One such experience happened for me on a spring morning in Cairo. An acquaintance from the Coptic Orthodox Church had come to take me on a tour of Cairo's Old City. In the mayhem of traffic, she was cut off from a desired exit and found herself going in the wrong direction. A string of police barricades separated our lane from the oncoming lane. Much to the annoyance of the line of cars behind us, she stopped to politely petition a policeman to open up the barricade, halt the oncoming flow of traffic, and let us make a U-turn in the middle of the road.

As she and the policeman discussed this request, the policeman's expression went from adamantly against to wavering. Unperturbed by the storm of horns and impatient voices that rained down upon us, my friend continued to negotiate as though what she was asking were well within his power to give. Suddenly his dark face broke into a broad smile and within seconds we had reversed our direction. "You just have to be nice to them," she said in a matter-of-fact tone.

It was one of those "lessons of life" moments that has stayed with me. There are many situations in life where we are literally in a jam. With a little creativity—thinking "outside the box" and acting with confidence and derring-do—we can turn things around and get them going in a positive direction.

A WINDOW OF ENTRY

Experience: Touring the ruins of Memphis, Egypt, 1981

I was standing amid the ruins of the ancient city of Memphis, which seemed to appear in the history of Egypt by virtue of some quantum leap from an unrecorded to a very high level of civilization. Represented today by the ramshackle village of Mit Rahina, Memphis perplexed me. Recalling the poor huts that my guide Marie and I had passed along the Nile, looking at the poverty of Mit Rahina, and trying to reconstruct in my mind the remains of the once-great temple of Ptah in which we stood, I wondered aloud what had happened to this great people and their civilization. Marie's response provided me with a way of thinking optimistically about new possibilities, even while standing amid ruins.

"Just stand here quietly," she said, "and feel the sacred energy that still hangs in the air. This place was once a revered contact point between the Divine and the people who inhabited this land. The Energy-Source that inspired among them such creative and lasting works of the human spirit is still available, can still be tapped into. What is needed for a new, rich merging is a window of entry through which that eternal and creative Spirit can electrify this people in this time.

All the essential ingredients are still here. With the right combination of vision, faith, and leadership, what happened can burst forth again—if not here, then somewhere else on our planet. This temple, even in this state of ruin, is a sign of the potential available to us."

☙

Twenty years later, standing before the ruins of the Temples of Agrigento in Sicily, I remembered Marie's words. From what lay before me came the question: what do I want to do with the possibilities represented in the brief span of time and energy allotted to me?

The Reminder of Ruins

This pile of pillars lying pell-mell in pieces
once stood proud and permanent
on the brow of the hill, marble-covered
columns, chiseled and gleaming
in Mediterranean light.

Six men with hands joined could not encircle
this section of column thrusting upward
from the rubble, only one of thirty-four
moved into place by some marvel
of ropes and pulleys to hold aloft
a roof over the temple of Zeus.

These stones have endured the hammers
and been pulled by the horses
of Phoenicians, Carthaginians, Romans, and Greeks;

provided prayerful sanctuary
for Moors bowing towards mecca
and Norman knights to the cross.

And now, scattered like fallen giants
in fields of wild grass, Sunday strollers zigzag
among them, reading in their large script
a reminder that the page on which they
presently step will soon be turned by
the finger of time.

What path, then, do you choose to walk
with your short and treasured life?

SHOOTS OF CREATIVITY

As I reflect on these scenes of my life experience, it becomes clear to me that my creative development runs roughly parallel to my years with the Paulists. There were crocus shoots piercing the earth before then: I acted in plays in both high school and college, and edited our literary magazine in college. But it wasn't until my years of graduate theology with the Paulists that those shoots of creativity began to grow and their petals open during the years following ordination.

I see something now I did not see then: the ecumenical and inter-faith work that took early root in my ministry, and gradually took over the whole of it, has been like a fertilizer spread over the soil of my adult life. The support and encouragement I have received in my community to give my life to this work has been like a greenhouse atmosphere surrounding growing plants. The Paulist community has provided the space, freedom, and support to become who I am, and for that, I shall be eternally grateful.

Each of us has a life map. How fascinating it would be if we could tell our stories with visual topographical aids, if we could materialize them three-dimensionally and actually see represented there the foothills and valleys, the desert treks and summit peaks, the forests and lakes of our lived experiences. But it is enough that we can identify them and their spiritual, emotional, psychological, and intellectual effects upon us.

What might making a map of your creative journey do for you? It might effect an interior shift in the way you perceive and respond to the events, people, and opportunities that come into your life. Such a shift is of no small consequence, and could well be the most important part of your experience with this book.

Your map needn't be a world map of far-flung places, nor a philosophical tome of lofty ideals, to be of value. What it must be is a map of *your* experiences, of the people and events in your life that have changed your angle of living. You can start by simply naming people and events that have opened you to new possibilities. However you might represent your creative journey, there are experiences in your life story that have acted like steroids to your imagination and sense of vocation, causing them to grow stronger with each new vision and possibility.

The late poet and potter M. C. Richards wrote, "The creative spirit creates with whatever materials are present. With food, with children, with building blocks, with speech, with thoughts, with pigment, with an umbrella, or a wineglass, or a blowtorch." Mapping is a way to look at what is "present" in your life, to recognize what has been and is creatively satisfying for you—whether done with a computer or dump truck, a public relations brochure or a kitchen stove. That's the place to start—with whoever *you* are.

One of the gifts of midlife is being able reflect on your life, to look back at things you've done, to acknowledge not only the things you feel good about and of which you are proud but also the hard places and rough roads that have shaped who you are and cultivated your creative spirit.

Once, during a trip to South Africa, I had the opportunity to visit the infamous prison on Robben Island where I met a woman whose life map held a striking place: the prison where Nelson Mandela was held. His long sojourn was something that had shaped her life journey—her values, her choices. As she looked back on her life, this was a location she never wanted to forget and from which she drew continual inspiration. Her visitations there helped her make the most of the opportunities she had as she faced her future.

Robben Island

It was so small, barely eight by ten,
cynically color-coordinated:
gray bedroll to match the steel-gray prison bars,
metal plate and cup.

Now the South Africans call him Madiba,
a term of endearment: father of the nation, great soul,
but for eighteen years he was number 00164.

The young woman next to me,
her skin as dark as the letters "Africa"
emblazoned across her shirt,
stood staring, unembarrassed by the tears
moistening her face,
gripping the bars,
weeping audibly now.

Her third visit, she confided;
a working mother in her 20s,

spending 100 rand to visit a prison
on her day off.

When I was growing up, she said,
and becoming militant,
Robben Island was a dirty word
around our house.
Whenever I would do something of which
my very conservative parents did not approve
they would say:
Do you want to go to Robben Island?
And now my answer is
Yes, I do!

Each time I come here, she said,
it helps my healing, it helps me forgive.
We are all in awe of Madiba's ability
to resist recrimination and bitterness
in offering those who were his captors
the hand of forgiveness and compassion.

He is our teacher.
I am getting ready to bring my three-year-old daughter
here. I want her to know this place
as a shrine of her freedom,
as a testimony to the triumph of the human spirit
over the forces of evil.

She dried her eyes with a tissue from her purse.

The work of becoming free is never done,

she said, the struggle never finished.

For each of us,

it is always a work in progress.

We could each say the same of our creative journey, of our efforts to become free from our insecurities and fears: "It is always a work in progress." As Joseph Allegretti points out in his book *Loving Your Job, Finding Your Passion*, once we acknowledge to ourselves that we *are* creative people who *do* creative work, we will begin to see more and more ways to express our creativity.

That prompts me to add two important points about making your own creativity journey map. First, it will always be changing because your journey is always continuing. And, second, your map is not a map in the traditional sense, made for others to follow to find their way. It is more like a private "treasure map," leading you to deeper discovery about yourself and what is close to your heart.

QUESTIONS FOR REFLECTION

What is the first time you can remember feeling awe?

Name three people who have inspired you by stretching your imagination, by expanding what you thought you were capable of doing.

What experiences in your life have given you new vision and energy?

What experiences have given you a sense of the presence of the Creative Spirit in the world?

EXERCISE TO ACCESS YOUR CREATIVITY

Set aside a generous block of time so you can thoughtfully begin to map your creative journey. It may be helpful to have a large surface (table, white board) to work on, or you may prefer using a computer so you can insert thoughts at random. However you choose to chart your journey, give yourself some flexibility for later inserts. You may find it helpful to use this chapter's "Questions for Reflection" as a starting point. Remember: there are no rules for making this map, no "right" or "wrong" way to do this. It is your life, your map. However you approach this exercise, my hope is that you will get a better sense of the seeds of creativity sown in your life, how their "roots" have already taken hold—and the untended shoots that have yet to blossom.

Inner Freedom

I want to be like
that rooster
made of metal
standing alert on one leg
atop a pinnacled roof
stopping between engagements
looking and listening
equipoised
to move in the direction
the breath of God
next blows.

FOUR

Four Paths to Develop Your Creativity

There is a cosmic dance of life going on all around us, but so often we are like people asleep in front of the television while a live parade passes by outside. We may complain about being "too involved," but in reality we are usually under- rather than over-involved. Our busyness reflects a condition of being scattered more than of being engaged. Slowly yielding ourselves to genuine involvement is the gateway to creativity.

Every summer, when I arrive at the lake island where I make a week's retreat, I need to slow down so I can wake up to the marvels of what is there. The way I begin is simply by sitting in the grass under a tree and looking closely at things.

The Cosmic Dance

The sun slides lower in the August sky
with beams of light dancing on the water

like glittering diamonds in exuberant display,
their movements dazzling the eye as they gather
and disperse, leaping and bobbing in all directions
to silent music flowing through the golden light.
Ants scurrying pell-mell on the ground
and bees zigzagging around my head
also seem to hear it, as does mother
with her ducklings passing by in a line dance
of webbed feet, and wren in the bush
darting and diving and fluttering her wings.

There is a Buddhist story about a disciple who was always complaining to his master, "You are hiding the final secret of Zen from me." And he would not accept his master's denials. One day they were walking in the hills when they heard a bird sing.

"Did you hear that bird sing?" asked the master.

"Yes," said the disciple.

"Well, now you know that I have hidden nothing from you."

Thus it was that the Buddha responded to his disciple's question: "What difference has being enlightened made in your life?"

"Well, when I eat, I eat. When I look, I look. When I listen, I listen."

"But everybody does that!" the disciple exclaimed.

"If everybody does that," the master rejoined, "then everybody is enlightened!"

This story captures the essence of the call to creativity: to awake to the marvel of what is there, to be fully engaged. Although there are many different ways to open this gateway, I have found the exercises, such as making a map, proposed by Dan Wakefield in his book *Releasing the Creative Spirit: Unleash the Creativity in Your Life* (SkyLight Paths) to be especially effective in my own life. Here I have adopted four of them that I hope will lead you to some new discoveries as well:

- Come to your senses
- Visit your special places
- Discover your music
- Seek inspiration from others

PATH 1: COME TO YOUR SENSES

We rarely give our full attention to *anything*. In our chronic multitasking, we skim the surface of everything: the headline news, the day's e-mail, the taste of food, the background music. If the headphones are not on, the television is. If we're not advancing what's on the computer screen while we talk on the telephone, we're shuffling papers on the desk or preparing some dish in the kitchen. We have lost touch with how satisfying it can be simply to be fully present to one thing. That, in effect, is the Zen of living. Less *is* more.

Experiencing anything with the headlights of awareness switched to "high beam" can be utterly captivating and enlivening. Petting a kitten, watching snow fall, tasting homemade soup, listening to birdsong, smelling the coffee or herbal tea. Life is a cornucopia of delights daily poured out for our pleasuring. The country has its palette of colors, and the city its density of faces and sounds. Everywhere the dazzling manifestation of creation, everywhere inspiration for the taking. The richness of life is unveiled simply by coming to our senses.

Always Start with Nothing

Always start with nothing
with your eyes closed
standing still
like you've never seen
or heard or touched
anything before.

Let the light come slowly in
and the images take shape.
Let your jaw drop in wonder
at the cumulus cloud
piled up like billowy fleece
against an extravagance
of blue velour whose end
you cannot see.

Let your breathing stop
in disbelief
as you press down naked feet
on blossoms of clover
and walk aimlessly
through a riot zone
of wildflowers whose names
you'll never know.

Let the follicles in your ears
come erect in rapt attention
at the notes of music
perfectly sung
by that wild, feathered thing
which just landed
in a pyramid of green.

Let the buds in your mouth
swell at the prospect
of incising those circles
of red, yellow, orange or green
that mysteriously hang
by fragile stems and
pendulate alluringly in the wind.

Let your nose and lungs fill
with the ambrosial perfume
of a wine-colored rose
and come to, looking up,
astonished at how
something so delicate
could put you
flat on your back
in the grass.

To open to a world of wonder,
simply start with nothing

Nothing releases the energy and delight of living—and the energy of creativity—more than coming to our senses. Literally. An essential ingredient of creative living is to unmuzzle our senses—or resuscitate them if they have been numbed by work or cacophonous noise or overeating or overdrinking. The Buddhists have it right in emphasizing wakefulness, mindfulness.

There is a story of a disciple who emerged from a period of silent retreat and went to meet with his master. When he arrived, he sat down and took from his bag a tangerine and peeled it, handing half of it to the master. Then, as he popped a section into his mouth, he began relating his experiences while on retreat. But the master said to him, "Let's just enjoy the tangerine first. Then we will talk."

Granted, if we took this approach every time we ate with others, there wouldn't be much time for conversation. But it would be beneficial if there were *some* meals that we ate with full attention. In the experience of attentiveness, the creative spirit is released.

There is much we can learn about attentiveness from other cultures and traditions. In the Japanese tea ceremony, for example, attention is the core component of the ritual. In preparing the tea, the host pays attention to the fire and the water, but especially to the spoon and the bamboo whisk. The spoon for measuring the powdered tea and the whisk for stirring it both require care and delicacy to ensure a perfect balance. When the proper measures of tea and boiled water are poured into the clay cups and stirred with the whisk until exactly right, visitors lift the cups, using both hands, feeling the texture and warmth. They drink the tea, not in one gulp, but in small sips, savoring the refreshing liquid. The purpose of the ritual is to be fully "there."

Another Japanese practice that cultivates full attention is the writing of haiku poetry. A classic haiku is a brief seventeen-syllable poem in three lines that holds up a mirror to nature and captures an image so fully that the reader immediately grasps the sense of the moment. Writing haiku poetry is an effective way of cultivating "present mind," of being awake to the sacrament of the moment. When I've tried my hand at it, as with these few haiku poems I wrote at an island retreat, I've been amazed by how much this poetic discipline challenges me to look more closely at things.

wind on the water

dancing branches in the pines

raindrops give warning

mist-covered mountains
vapor rising off the lake
hushed holy sunrise

rose-colored water
and clouds of baked salmon
sunset feast for all

There is a Zen proverb that says, "Before enlightenment, chop wood, carry water. After enlightenment, chop wood, carry water." The action may be the same both before and after, but the interior experience of the action after enlightenment is qualitatively different. From a similar slant, one of my favorite definitions of contemplative prayer is "taking a long, loving look at the Real." Daily life may appear the same externally, but its inner quality changes when our perceptions change. And looking more closely at things may well be the simplest, most effective way of shifting our perspective and awakening our creativity. As the expert on mysticism Evelyn Underhill once observed, the artist is essentially a contemplative who has learned to express herself and who relates her soul-fire in color, speech, or sound.

When we live with our senses fully awake, every day can be a "Circus Day":

Today is going to be a circus day!
Today you get to feel velvety water on human skin,
listen to music standing smack between two speakers,
squeeze the last drops from the grapefruit
straight into your mouth
warm your hands around a hot mug
and experience how good it feels to pee.

And those are just the preliminary events!

In the skydome you can
watch the chickadees dive and swoop but never crash,
squint at sunbeams tap dancing on sparkling water,
applaud teams of ants pulling four times
their weight,
catch the illusions in sunlight and shadows,
and witness clouds changing before
your very eyes.

And get this: there's no admission!
You only have to show up
awake.

PATH 2: VISIT YOUR SPECIAL PLACES

We experience places almost the way we do people. Some we immediately love, while others make us uncomfortable. Sometimes our first impression of a place will change as we spend more time in it. And our reactions to places are as personal to ourselves as our reactions to people. Just because I like a particular town or village or restaurant is no guarantee that it will be on the list of favorites of others in my circle of friends. In seeking to cultivate our creativity, it is important to know which places get our creative juices flowing.

One sweet spot on the planet for me is an island in the middle of Lake George in upstate New York. The lake is thirty-six miles long and narrow, walled by the Adirondack Mountains. Smack in the middle of it, right where the mountains are highest, floats a cluster of wild and windblown islands identified as a group on the map as the Harbor Islands. But among the members of my community, each has its own name. In 1871 the leadership of the community acquired them, named them after our founders, and subsequently built a chapel on one of them (Hecker Island) and a bunkhouse cabin on another (Hewitt Island). There is no electricity—just the sun and the water, the wind and the waves, the mountains and the stars. Daily, there is a "Free Concert":

> *A free concert tonight,*
> *woodwinds blowing from the south*
> *and great waves percussing upon the rocks,*
> *bats and night owls in full flight.*
>
> *Listen closely and you'll hear the crickets*
> *keeping rhythm with their chimes*
> *and the bullfrog with his tuba in the thickets*
> *by the bay.*
>
> *Who arranges their invisible score*
> *with no conductor on the floor*
> *in a symphony hall that takes no tickets,*
> *has no ceiling, walls, or door?*

From the minute I set foot on the wild grass and climb up onto the shelf of rocks that gives the best view down the lake, my inner spirit takes a deep bow. When I am in that zone of light and air, it is as though my soul rises up like a genie from a bottle opened, and my pores expand to let it out. Although I have been blessed to travel around the world, well over half of my poems have been born on that island.

This Is the Place

This is the place
where I am ravished,
the place where my Love comes
with the stealth and mystery
of the full moon rising
over the mountains.

This is the place
where my heart bursts,
the place whose alluring beauty
is etched upon my soul,
where sleep is fathoms deeper
and waking is being born.

This is the place
where my compulsions molt and wither,
where I am a perennial initiate
in the mindful art of floating,
and warm to the joy of being
by baking on the rocks.

This is the place
where I have wrestled
with demons and with angels,
where the fibers of my soul
have been pulled outside my body
and worked between strong fingers.

This is the place
of my poetry and passion.
Like Jacob at Bethel,
I have awoken here
and whispered:

"Truly, truly,
the Lord is in
this place.
I will build an altar
  here."

Our creative energies also flow in places where we feel deeply at home. When we are there, we sleep better, laugh more deeply, concentrate more easily. Work in that place, whether mental or manual, feels more like a pastime because we do it in a relaxed manner. For me, in such a place prayer comes as naturally as floating.

Morning Prayer

Morning prayers are best said
in the water, belly-up,
facing the rising sun,
and immersed in the
renewing feel of the font
with your ears submerged
so that everything you say
is magnified, flying straight up
to be heard by all the trees

and the mountains
and to be carried away on the wind
by the ravens and the gulls
for the rest of the world.

There are other places where the energy field is so rich and palpable that everyone who enters into it is marked by it. To borrow Angeles Arrien's statement in *The Second Half of Life*, oftentimes the most excellent expression of our inner wilderness is the wilderness of nature. Indigenous cultures and spiritual traditions consider water, woods, mountains, and deserts natural sanctuaries where we can come home to who we are. For native peoples, these are places of rebirth and renewal. Nature (from the Latin *natus*, "to be born") is, in its majesty and tranquility, a balm to our souls and opens inner gateways to contemplation, reflection, integration, and transformation. Such wild places can open us to the mysterious promptings of our own vast inner world, of our most hidden creative self.

Several years ago a group of family members and friends whitewater rafted through almost two hundred miles of the Grand Canyon over a week's time. When we weren't shooting the rapids on the Colorado River, we were exploring side canyons, bathing in the waterfalls, jumping into pools, baking on the sun-heated rocks. By night we slept in the sand under the stars on slivers of beaches. It was a magical time in an enchanted place that made it possible to conceive even of death in romantic, adventurous images.

I want to die
by the friendly fire
of shooting stars.
I want to go
with my eyes wide open,

watching the free-flowing
current carry me, swirling,
around the bend to where
the river drops out of sight
in singing, sundancing
crests of white.

As one group member described the power of this place, "It is forever imprinted on the emulsion sheet of my mind." She spoke for us all. Some places on the planet are extraordinary and leave no one indifferent. They are places of power that touch and stir our creativities.

One such place for me is Mount Athos in northern Greece. Athos is an isolated, mountainous peninsula that stretches into the Aegean Sea between the Thermaic and Strimonic Gulfs. As the hillocks of the landward end extend seaward, clusters of peaks swell higher and higher to finally reach their apex in the bare slopes of Mount Athos, whose pyramid-shaped summit rises sheer from the sea to more than six thousand feet.

The peninsula is punctuated with twenty large monasteries—daring buildings, really; marvels of monastic architecture that perch on cliffs like eagles' nests high above the sea. At the furthermost point of the peninsula, on wild cliffs rising straight from the sea, live the ascetics and hermits, seemingly beyond any connection with the world as we know it. Chain ladders lead up from the sea to isolated huts, rickety cottages, and caves, which ensure the hermits' peace and isolation.

The monasteries themselves are like living museums richly stocked with artistic treasures of the Byzantine past, and the true Byzantine-style of worship has been preserved in its pristine form. The whole of the living tradition on this "Holy Mountain" is a sacred repository for the understanding of theology, philosophy, history, Byzantine and post-Byzantine art, and Eastern mysticism. It is a mesmerizing world unto itself, a hallowed atmosphere that spins its spell around anyone who visits. When I first stood on these cliffs, looking out over the placid sea at sunset, I found myself thinking that urban traffic jams and fast-food restaurants and rock concerts might be only residual memories from a dream.

Another very special place on the planet for me is the Iona Abbey in Scotland. I had heard and read much about this place, and one year, when I finished up leading a retreat in Ireland, I decided to make a pilgrimage to this tiny island. Iona is a small isle about three miles long and one-and-a-half miles wide off the west coast of Scotland where, in 563, Columba founded a Celtic monastery. In 975 it was sacked by Viking raiders, but it was rebuilt and reinhabited by European Benedictines in the twelfth century. After World War I, Rev. George MacLeod, a visionary Presbyterian parish minister in Glasgow, saw the ruins of the abbey as a symbol of European civilization. He called Protestants and Catholics, clergy and laypeople, to work together in restoring it as a sign of hope for the future.

Today Iona Abbey, completely rebuilt, is at the heart of a nonresidential ecumenical Christian community of men and women (200 members, 1,500 associate members, and around 1,700 friends) from many backgrounds and denominations who are committed to a rule of living that involves daily scripture reading, sharing and accounting for their use of time and money, action for justice and peace, and regular meetings with other members in their area. Running through all their engagements is a commitment to strengthening interdenominational understanding and the promotion of interfaith dialogue. The current character of Iona Abbey and its history offer an ongoing source of inspiration to pilgrims from around the world.

In Celtic spirituality, places such as the Iona Abbey, where an experience of the Transcendent seeps through the membrane between the material and the spiritual worlds, are called "thin" places. When we are in these places our creative energies are on tiptoe, ready to dance.

To St. Columba and the Abbey of Iona

It must have been the evening light
that drew him here, this golden translucence
suffused with the soft, woolly warmth
of sheep flocks filling the fields.

Or it might have been the air at sunrise,
so clearly virgin to any soot or smog,
scented freshness arising from the sea.

Or was it the clouds, high peaks
of purest cotton precariously stacked
on the highland cliffs across the bay?

He was a saint, of course, but any
sinner could see that this is a thin place,
one of those sweet spots in the planet
where the membrane separating heaven
and earth is tissue-thin and porous,
where the crystalline light, emerald earth,
turquoise sea, and freshly minted air
all harmonize in chorus, enchanting the heart
and directing the seeker to build the temple
here.

As is often the case with our special places, we may live far from
them and only have access to them during special times of the year or

holidays. But there are still ways that we can tap into the raw power of these energy fields in our normal living throughout the year. One of my confreres painted a picture for me of an empty chair under my favorite pine tree on Hewitt Island from the perspective of looking down the lake with the mountains descending on both sides. I had it framed and it now hangs over the dresser in my room where I stand and look at it every day before opening the drawer and initiating the quotidian realities with socks and underwear. I want to gather some of the creative energy that I know is in that place. Until I can sit in that chair again and give my spirit free and full indulgence, I cherish the memory and glean from it fresh energy for the canvas of the day ahead.

What Happens to the Human Spirit

What happens to the human spirit
when noise from planes overhead
and traffic on the ground,
from factories and sirens
and cement mixers turning round,
throw a cover over natural sounds
and make it impossible to hear
barking, birdsong, evening breezes
and brush rustled by deer?

The effect is largely the same
as in a garden without rain:
imagination serves up pale,
withered fruits, and the mind
grows thoughts with shallower roots;

whereas things natural and wild
open the windows of the soul,
resurrect the wonder of a child
and sharpen clarity about the goal.

PATH 3: DISCOVER YOUR MUSIC

What is it about music that a single chord or two struck on a piano can immediately trigger the memory of a whole song? Sometimes only three or four notes instantly transport us to another time and place.

Dr. Daniel Levitin, a cognitive psychologist who runs the laboratory for Music Perception, Cognition and Expertise at McGill University in Montreal, has focused his attention on why music has such an intense effect upon us and how music affects our emotions. For Dr. Levitin, music is not just a cluster of sounds, but an art with which we interact.

In one of his first experiments, he stopped people on the street and asked them to sing, entirely from memory, one of their favorite songs. The results were astonishingly accurate. Most people could hit the tempo of the original song within a 4 percent margin of error, and two-thirds sang within a semitone of the original pitch, a level of accuracy that wouldn't embarrass a pro.

"When [we] played the recording of them singing alongside the actual recording of the original song," Levitin reported in a *New York Times* article, "it sounded like they were singing along." When you think about it, that's a remarkable feat. Most memories degrade and distort with time, but music memories remain sharply encoded in our brains. Music's effects on us are simply astonishing.

Consider, for example, how music can fill you up, change your mood, set your body moving, bring a smile to your face, or bring tears to your eyes. It can kidnap you in a time capsule and in the wink of an eye whisk you away and drop you onto a dance floor or a beach or into a church in a former life. It can make grown men drop their fears and march into battle, bring a whole crowd to their feet in spontaneous applause, or pull a depressed person back from the ledge of despair.

It has often been said that music is the language of the heart. No wonder, then, that there is a privileged pathway from the sound of music to the latent pool of our creative energies. No wonder music stirs the waters of imagination, evoking images and memories that are the stuff of stories and sculpture, laughter and love.

When I Go to an Indian Concert

When I go to an Indian concert
I'm looking for a feeling.
I want the sound of the sitar
to make my eyes roll back in my head
with lids lightly closed.

I want the dancer's almond eyes
and jangling ankle bells
to whisk me away
to the banks of the Ganges
where painted zadus sit in saffron robes
and graceful women come for water
wrapped in silk saris with flowers in their hair.

I want the singer's moaning melody
to transport me to temples
where the nostrils flare and twitch with incense
and the heart's yearning for

mystical communion with the Divine
burns like an oil lamp
before the Dance of Shiva.

Movement to music is such a universal phenomenon. My sister and I learned to rock 'n roll in our basement to the 50s sounds of Buddy Holly, Jimmy Rodgers, and Elvis Presley, and I have loved to dance ever since. No surprise, then, that one of the ways my creative energies began to find expression in the second half of my life was in response to music that touched my spirit. In my practice of yoga, I began to develop *vinyasa*, or "posture flows," to favorite prayers that had musical settings. Bach's "Our Father." Schubert's "Ave Maria." "The Breastplate of St. Patrick" by Shaun Davey. "The Peace Prayer of St. Francis" and the "Take Lord, Receive" of St. Ignatius, both by the St. Louis Jesuits. I began praying them not just with my mind but also with my whole being. I would let the music enter and fill my heart, and then begin to give expression to my feelings with my body. The physicality of this body prayer was new for me, and it unleashed powerful energy.

I am reminded of something that Felix Mendelssohn once said: "Though everything else may appear shallow and repulsive, even the smallest task in music is so absorbing, and carries us so far away from town, country, earth, and all worldly things, that it is truly a blessed gift of God." Little did I realize at the time how far this "task in music" would carry me!

A friend happened to be visiting from out of town, and as we were doing yoga together one morning, she asked if I would share with her how I prayed through the postures. I put on a favorite song prayer and "embodied" it, as had become my daily practice.

When it was over, she sat silently on the floor for a long while with tears running down her face. Finally she spoke: "As you did that, pieces of things started coming together inside me. Something that has been slowly evolving within me over the years just took a great leap forward and found conscious expression in your prayer. My heart was saying 'yes! Yes! YES!'"

Gradually I began to introduce these music-movement prayers into my yoga classes. People loved them, learned them, took them home, and started integrating them into their own prayer lives. I encouraged them to let the Creator Spirit move within their own hearts and to "choreograph" their own prayers.

Eventually I began giving "Prayer of Heart and Body" retreats in which I introduced people to praying in this way. Then one day a company called Sounds True, which produces audio and video resources, contacted me from out of the blue and said, "We've been following what you are doing and think you're really on to something. Would you be interested in making it available more widely in video format?"

A month later I met with a company representative. When I suggested that she might find it helpful to see exactly what it was that I was doing, she agreed. I asked if we could spend a few moments in silence together first, since I was about to do something very intimate: I was going to pray in her presence.

After collecting ourselves, she started the music and I prayed in the way I have come to pray every morning upon rising—in a sequence of embodied song prayers. When the music stopped, we both sat in stillness again for a few minutes.

She finally broke the silence and said, "I *want* that video! I want it first of all for myself!"

The resulting video project ultimately gave birth to the *Yoga Prayer* DVD, in which music, prayers, and yoga postures are offered in a unique spiritual practice. What had started out for me as simply an experiment in listening and responding to music had become a creative expression beyond anything I had ever imagined. I think of them now as body-poems because I've noticed that when I'm expressing the prayer's heart sentiments through movement to music, I experience the same energizing feeling as when I'm writing a poem. My physical connection with the music opened me not only to new creative energy but also to new avenues of sharing and encouraging creativity.

There is a story told of how God, upon banishing Adam and Eve from the Garden of Eden, called all the angels together and asked if any of them would volunteer to leave the Garden and go with Adam and Eve so they would never forget the glories of paradise and would be continually reminded of their destiny. There was silence among the angels and no one moved, for they were all reluctant to leave such a place. Finally one angel stepped forward and raised a wing. "Ahhh," God said, smiling, "I was hoping it would be you!"

It was the angel of music.

PATH 4: SEEK INSPIRATION FROM OTHERS

When I was eight or nine, I was a regular visitor at the public library. Mrs. Miller, who sat at the desk, knew me well. Like clockwork I would appear on Saturday mornings to return one of the Hardy Boys mysteries and check out another. I went right down the shelf until I'd read them all. They introduced me to a world of intrigue and adventure, of camaraderie and daring. (There was some relationship, I'm sure, between the exciting world in my imagination and the difficulty my parents were having in keeping me in school. Compared to my imaginary adventures with the Hardy Boys, school seemed pretty dull and boring.)

In college I would sit for long hours in the language lab listening to Shakespearean tragedies and comedies, emerging intellectually invigorated by the richness and musicality of the language. In literature class I thrilled to the creativity of e. e. cummings and the way he broke all the rules and exploded images like landmines in the middle of a sentence, giving words a whole new dynamism.

I remember vividly when I first saw the movie *Chariots of Fire*; it was a preview matinee showing in February. This compelling story of two British athletes training for and competing in the 1924 Summer

Olympics lit such a fire in me that, when I came out, I walked straight home, changed my clothes, grabbed my cross-country skis, and headed for Mount Royal Park two blocks away. In the waning hours of the afternoon, I skied forty kilometers on a hilly terrain nonstop before the sun set. I connected so powerfully with the story that the energy just kept gushing up like a freshly struck oil well deep within.

Live theater evokes a similar response in me. I thrilled to the splendid Broadway revival of the *Man of La Mancha*. Watching certain scenes, I was aware that my nostrils were flaring and my eyes blurring with tears, and I wanted to stand up in the audience and, with conviction and verve, sing along with Don Quixote in "To Dream the Impossible Dream."

Whether it is the use of percussive instruments in the play *Stomp*, the song and dance numbers in the musical *Mamma Mia!*, the vocal harmonies in *Jersey Boys*, the humor in *Hairspray* and *Wicked*, the costumes in *The Lion King*, the finely balanced argument in *Doubt*, the razor-sharp repartee in *Dirty Rotten Scoundrels*, or the innovative interpretation of classics such as *The Crucible* and *Fiddler on the Roof*, the sheer creativity of live theater is an ongoing source of inspiration for me.

During my seven years in New York City, living within a five-minute walk of Lincoln Center for the Performing Arts, I developed a love affair with the ballet. Whether the longer, integral ballets, such as *Swan Lake*, *Raymonda*, or *Sylvia*, or the shorter variety programs, such as *The Red Violin*, *Le Baiser de la Fée*, or the *Vienna Waltzes*, the invention, freshness, and feeling of the combined music and movement is always extraordinary to me.

One evening, after seeing *Liebeslieder Walzer*, in which the music by Johannes Brahms (*Opus 52* and *Opus 65*) is danced to choreography by George Balanchine, I was so stimulated that I knew I would not be able to lie down and sleep, even though it was eleven o'clock and past my normal bedtime. So I gathered the creative energies that were whirling within into this poem:

The Ballet

Nothing buoys my spirit like the ballet
where these magicians of movement
explore the boundaries of outer space,
leaping, flying, human gliders
in an aesthetic of elegance and grace.

They whirl and twirl like tops spun round,
wrapped in gowns of satin and lace,
twirling to the ethereal orchestral sound
in pure movement, leaving no trace
in thin air, sharply sculpted on the ground.

And that lithesome divine being who stands
on one toe and points the other at the moon,
she makes me swoon with her flutter of hands
and her intricate flows so fully in tune
with her partner, now trapped by her bands

of seduction and desire. Let the curtain fall,
it makes no matter, their dance of fire
will make me stand up tall outside the hall
for I share their race and from the choir
sing of how they do the rest of us inspire.

These are the wells of inspiration we need to return to when
we're feeling beaten down and it's all we can do just to get out of bed

in the morning. These are the sparks that can relight a creative fire in us. Dipping back into such wellsprings is not only fun and pleasurable, but it can also invigorate the mind, body, and soul.

If you're feeling dry and in need of inspiration, revisit the wells that have nurtured your imagination in earlier times. Read again from the novels that kept you up late at night because you couldn't put the books down. Bring home a video of a Broadway musical that lifted your spirit and put a spring back into your step. Sift through the post-cards of your holiday in Paris until you find the sculpture of Rodin's *The Kiss* that touched you so deeply. Play the songs you love to sing along with. Call a friend and go dancing.

Let the inspiration of others bring you back into the realm of your own passion and dreams.

QUESTIONS FOR REFLECTION

Which of your senses would you say is most acute? What pleasures do you derive from this sense? With what emotions does this sense link you? What kinds of experiences are most likely to awaken this sense in you?

What is your current relationship with nature? Which of its sanctuaries most draw you—mountains, deserts, waters, or woods? What are some of the places that wake up or stretch your dormant creative energies? When was the last time you visited one of these places?

Is music important to you? Does it mean more or less to you with the passing of the years? If you listed half a dozen pieces of music or songs that stir your soul, what would they be? When was the last time you went dancing or in some way let yourself move to music?

What movies, plays, athletic performances, books, pieces of music, poems, or other works of art have inspired you?

EXERCISES TO ACCESS YOUR CREATIVITY

Come to Your Senses

I occasionally give this exercise to retreat participants and instruct them to return at an appointed time to share with one another what they have written. They are often astonished by what comes out of themselves. Try it yourself and see what happens.

> 1. Take a leisurely stroll, stopping to look at things.
>
> 2. When something in particular engages you, take ten minutes to study it closely. Pay special attention to each of your senses: What details do you see? Do you hear anything? What can you smell? What are your physical sensations?
>
> 3. Take another ten minutes to describe it in detail in writing.
>
> 4. Then, write down what emotions this "full attention" evokes in you.
>
> 5. Finally, use what you have written to create a poem. (Let me anticipate your protest, "But I'm not a poet!" Just see what happens. Let the words emerge in any way that feels authentic for you.)

Visit Your Special Places

Open your calendar and mark off some occasions when you could spend some time in a place that brings you alive.

Discover Your Music

Check the local paper for listings of live music performances in your area and select one to attend. When you go, pay particular attention to your emotional and physical responses to the music.

Seek Inspiration from Others

Is there a friend or relative who is accomplished at something you would like to learn or try? Ask him or her to show you how to do it.

On Flying a Kite

Speak to me of life,
of challenge and adversity, I cried,
and later that day stepped with fragile craft
out into the wind.

But going   with
the consoling breeze
gave no loft.
Designed to ride the currents of the air,
the winged thing only hopped along,
rising and falling
rising and falling
dragging the tail of rainbow-colored ribbons
through puddles and grass.

Then I turned   against
the wind
and the puny creature soared
billowing out
leaping straight up
reaching for the clouds
quickly running out the string.

And the rainbow of ribbons
bobbed and danced
scribbling its wisdom on the whiteboard of the clouds:
resistance draws us to our noblest heights.

FIVE

Four Practices to Tap into Your Creative Potential

Have you ever seen the play (or the movie) *Man of La Mancha*? It is based on the universally known picaresque romance *Don Quixote* by the sixteenth-century writer Miguel de Cervantes Saavedra. Cervantes, who wrote forty plays in twenty years, all of them failures, was excommunicated from the Church and served several jail terms on various charges. Aging and infirm, he wrote *Don Quixote* to try to make some money.

Librettist Dale Wasserman hit on the idea of combining the stories of Cervantes and Quixote. What kind of man, Wasserman wondered, could suffer unceasing failures and yet in his declining years produce the staggering testament to the human spirit that is *Don Quixote*? Wasserman answered his own question by casting a play within a play. I'm going to take a few moments here to summarize the plotline because I believe it has many key insights into this whole business of creativity.

Man of La Mancha opens with Cervantes in prison, awaiting trial by the Inquisition. The prisoners have decided to hold a mock trial in order to find him guilty and steal what seems to be a valuable package—which, in fact, is the manuscript of Cervantes's novel, *Don Quixote*.

When asked, "What is your crime?" Cervantes responds, "I am a poet."

In an effort to save his work, Cervantes proposes to present his argument in the form of a play. The "court" agrees, and Cervantes is determined to win his case by putting the prisoners in touch with their poetic souls. By engaging them in the play, he hopes they can gain access to a part of themselves that has truly been "in prison."

Donning costume and makeup, Cervantes plays the role of a country squire named Alhonso, who has decided to transform himself into "Don Quixote," a knight on a quest. As Don Quixote, he leaves what society considers sane behavior to dedicate himself to righting the wrongs of the world and to call people to accept their inner gifts, which they no longer recognize.

On the road Don Quixote finds himself in a country tavern, where he encounters a barmaid named Aldonza, who appears to be the projection of his poetic soul—or his "inner feminine," to put it in Jungian terms. He sings to her, "I have dreamed thee too long … Thou hast always been with me but we have always been far apart."

The people in Don Quixote's life do everything they can to get him to "accept reality," to operate from the earn-your-living-and-be-sensible side of his mind. But he will not let go: "I come in a world of iron to make a world of gold." And he encourages them to have the courage to follow the quest for their own deepest longings, singing "the world will be better for this" in the song "To Dream the Impossible Dream."

Back in the real world of the prison, the inmates and the kanga-roo court are doing their best, as well, to get Cervantes to accept that real life is different from his poetic vision of it. One inmate tells Cervantes to write the visionary and the poetic out of his life, to throw away his manuscript, to douse the fire that burns within him.

As the play-within-a play continues, Don Quixote seems to have accepted this reality. The old man who had once tilted valiantly at windmills has returned home and is dying. He has cut off his creative self and is in the process of a lingering death of the soul. But his creative force, his intuitive feminine, fights back in the person of Aldonza, who insists on seeing him on his deathbed. She testifies how his living out of his creative self and his vision of the beauty and goodness in people has made a difference in her life. In a stirring deathbed scene, Don Quixote's poetic self and his practical self are reconciled, and he dies a whole person, going out in a blaze of glory.

Back in Cervantes's dungeon, his fellow prisoners are deeply affected by his story and restore to him his precious manuscript. When Cervantes is summoned to his real trial by the Inquisition, the prisoners unite to sing him on his way with "The Impossible Dream."

I think one of the reasons *Man of La Mancha* enjoyed such a long run on Broadway (and later in movie form) is that it touches a place deep within us where we know there are more possibilities to our lives than we are living. This classic adventure suggests that we, too, can live our "impossible dream" if we take to heart the practice of tapping our creative potential. I would like to propose these four practices in particular:

- Listen to your longings
- Have your own experience
- Work the edge of your comfort zone
- Surrender to the adventure

PRACTICE 1: LISTEN TO YOUR LONGINGS

I saw *Man of La Mancha* again in its Broadway revival in 2004, and I periodically watch it in its movie version. Each time it provides me with fresh encouragement to get in touch with my inner longings. Don Quixote would have us believe that if we feed and nourish our longings in whatever way we can, then our longings do the work and will gradually move us in new directions—*if we listen to them.*

I knew a real-life Don Quixote: the English Benedictine Bede Griffiths, known primarily for his work as a pioneer in interfaith dialogue in India. Father Bede spent the better part of his life consciously seeking a balance between his thirst for solitude and his gift for communication, integration of reason and intuition, and, most of all, reconciliation between the masculine and the feminine in his own person.

He knew that the scales were seriously imbalanced: he inhabited a masculine world both environmentally (the monastery) and temperamentally (living in the intellect, abstaining from any expression of sexual feelings). When he went to India at age forty-nine, he wrote to a friend that he was drawn there by the need to discover the other half of his soul, the feminine dimension that he felt was lacking in the Western world and in the Western Church.

For most of his life that search went forward more on a theoretical than on a real plane, for the experience of his feminine side eluded him. He was eighty-four when his Quixotic quest for integration of these opposing dimensions of himself culminated in a way nobody could have foreseen.

While sitting on the veranda of his thatched hut at his Christian ashram in south India early on a January morning in 1990, he felt a tremendous explosion within his head that seemed to lift his chair right off the ground. He managed to make it to his bed, where one of his monks later found him. The medical diagnosis was congestive heart failure, pulmonary edema, and a slight stroke.

Father Bede improved slowly and within a month was reading and writing and seeing a few visitors. He spent hours and hours reflecting on what had happened to him. Then, about a month later, he had another episode of intense pressure in his head and thought he was dying. The inspiration came suddenly to "surrender to the Mother." When he did, he experienced waves of love flowing into him, and he called out, "I am being overwhelmed by love."

Although he was aware that he had been touched at the core of his being, the process of change and understanding went on for months. A year later, when I spent a month at his ashram, he talked freely of it with great reverence. He spoke of it as being the awakening of his repressed feminine side, which demanded attention and integration. He could only explain it as an experience of God as Mother. He described "the feminine" appearing in forms of a black Madonna, as Earth Mother, as his own mother, as the fertile power of the womb, as Shakti (the feminine aspect of divine energy in Hindu understanding). He felt it was this feminine power that had struck him: "The left brain and whole rational system had been knocked down, and the right brain and the intuitive understanding, the sympathetic mind, had been opened up."

Bede lived for another two years to the day after his experience, and he said at one point that he had grown more in those two years than in the previous eighty-four. He was fascinated by this breakthrough to the feminine and all that it released in him: "God is not simply in the light, in the intelligible world, in the rational order. God is in the darkness, in the womb, in the Mother, in the chaos from which the order comes."

To grasp the link between our inner feminine and our inner longings, it is helpful to look once again at the writings of Carl Jung. He identified two polar opposites in our human nature: masculine (outer, conscious, rational, direct, assertive, outward-directed, practical) and feminine (inner, unconscious, intuitive, receptive, nurturing, inward-directed, creative). He warned of the dangers of overidentifying with either the outer or the inner world rather than integrating them. As long as we subjugate our intuitive, instinctive, and nonrational side in our need to explain everything rationally, we repress and deny whole areas of our human experience. As Father Bede insisted, in the years after age forty, we can address more directly what life is all about. Everything that comes before is preparation for the flowering of the whole personality.

Instead of choosing one world over the other, we have a chance to become adept at living in both. Jungian psychology is, in the final analysis, about the reconciliation of the opposites within us and the psychic energy that springs from the tension between these opposites. Allowing new capacities to come to awareness, seeing ourselves as more than we have yet been able to express, are critical steps in the process. It is the receptivity of our feminine side that allows us to open to our innermost longings.

Or to put it another way, as Sufi mystic Dr. Llewellyn Vaughan-Lee has written, "Longing is a highly dynamic state and yet at the same time it is a state of receptivity. *Because our culture has for so long rejected the feminine, we have lost touch with the potency of longing* [italics added for emphasis]."

Opening to our feminine side—to the womb of our deepest longings—is to call the soul back to its central place. And that is precisely what Aldonza did in *Man of La Mancha*: she called the dying man back to what was deepest and truest in him; she touched the longing in his soul that had created "Don Quixote."

It's one thing to understand this "listening to longing" in theory, but what does it look like in real life? What might we do to support this process of inner listening? What does this work of integrating the feminine and the masculine polarities look like in concrete terms? Where do we begin?

The medieval German theologian and mystic Meister Eckhart believed that the most powerful prayer and the worthiest work is the outcome of a quiet mind. To tap into our full creative potential, we need to stop and focus so we can drink in with our souls what is unfolding. It is in that interior, silent posture of paying attention that we will hear our inner longings most clearly.

One of the best ways I know to listen like this is to protect time for just sitting and looking with the mind in neutral. Befriend quiet. Turn off the music and the television. Take time to reflect. Allow yourself to *look* and *feel*. Create some contemplative space in which your deep longings can emerge. Listen to the unfulfilled desires that bubble up when sitting in a sauna or driving down the highway in silence.

Silence

A presence filled these walls last night.
It arrived earlier in the day
like slowly advancing fog,
a floating stillness.

By nightfall it had settled in
and wrapped itself around me
like a tender embrace,
placing gentle fingers on my eyes
and inviting me to feel the richness
of its presence from within.

When I awoke this morning
I looked into the still waters of the lake
and saw reflected there the secret, hidden depths
that lie within and only reveal their wisdom
to a quiet and listening heart.

PRACTICE 2: HAVE YOUR OWN EXPERIENCE

I thought of Father Bede's experience while walking on the beach in Florida during that serendipitous week with my parents, listening to David Whyte reflect on poetry.

The challenging thing about writing poetry, says Whyte, is that you must have your own experience, you must stop "remembering" life and start experiencing it directly, with all the switches turned on. He uses the Zen koan "Two hands clap and there is a sound; what is the sound of one hand?" to make his point:

> When we lose faith in our own voice and the natural speech arising from our bodies, we are like that one hand. We have no faith that our inner and outer worlds can meet. When the inner and outer worlds do meet like two hands clapping, you get a sharp, clear sound. This is your soul, your poem, your voice.

When Father Bede's inner and outer worlds met, it was the sound of two hands clapping. Prior to this life-changing experience, I don't believe he had lost faith in his own voice, but after it, he spoke with a new confidence from his sacred depth and with an assurance he had not possessed before. He was no longer the aged scholar "remembering life" but a person whose heart was profoundly touched by a direct experience of life, a person who spoke with freshness and conviction out of that experience.

What happened to Father Bede—and to the Don Quixotes of this world—is extraordinary only in the degree of voltage, not in the current itself. We are each called to have our own experience, to *feel* the current of life.

You

The Buddha said that receiving a human birth
is more rare than the chance that a blind turtle
floating in the ocean would stick his head through
  a small hoop.

So how will you practice gratitude today?
How seize the grace of conscious life,

how celebrate a mind that can know
   "this moment is like this"?

You poked your head through the hoop,
found the hole in the ice and surfaced. You
are given this short, precious time to know life
firsthand, to have your own experience. You
           get the privilege.
                You.

In making the most of this precious opportunity to know life firsthand, we need to not only *listen* but also *respond* to our longings, to the voice that rises from within asking to be heard. To put it bluntly, in order to *be* creative and to have our own experience, we need to actually *do* something.

This is not the kind of doing that needs planning ahead, as in, "Today, I'm going to be creative." I'm talking about being open to the response that longing spontaneously generates. Whenever we step into the gravity field of our longing, it can become so strong that we feel as if there is nothing else we can do but follow it. That is the very birthplace of creativity.

One of my confreres, Steve Bossi, had a bachelor's degree in political science and a master's in economics. To his parents' disappointment, he decided to enter the Peace Corps. While working in India, he saw from a new angle the immense influence of America in the world—how people there watch our television programs, go to our movies, and emulate our style of dress. Then he thought to himself, "If I can make the slightest contribution to American culture and economic policy, I can have an impact on the world." When he came back to the United States, he took a job in the U.S. Conference of Catholic Bishops' Social Development Department. While working on a national level, he met some inspiring priests and decided to become one. Today he directs the Paulist seminary and is forming leaders for the future. Imagine how different his story might be if he hadn't listened to his longings, if he had given into family pressure to go into business. His decision to "go for it" and have his own experience in the Peace Corps was a decision that held within it other unfoldings and led to where he is today.

I also think of my brother Kevin. He's a high school teacher and cross-country coach who encourages his runners to have their own experience. He accepts that some of them are just not built to be runners, but he tells them it's not only about their speed; it's also about togetherness, being outdoors, and working their edge. Whereas most coaches only keep "personal best" records, he also keeps records of the slowest ever to *finish* a race. Each year he dreams up a new theme for the season (this year's: "How much is enough?") and gives it to the team on T-shirts, not expecting a one-size-fits-all answer. He takes the team on a preseason camping trip ("First time some of these city kids have ever been in a sleeping bag") and has them do night walks in the woods without flashlights. When one of the parents asked him, "How is it that you have seventy kids on a *cross-country* team?" he responded, "We have fun!" He provides his athletes with venues for, and allows them to have, their own experience. And in the process, they discover capacities within themselves they never knew they had.

Your experiential response to longing might be something as simple as letting go of your travel plans when you find yourself in a place along the way that is everything you want a vacation to be. How many times have you been in a place, rejoiced in everything about it, and then left it for another much less satisfying place because some preordained schedule you had concocted for yourself said, "It's time to go now"?

Your response to longing might mean taking a day or a holiday to do something out of the ordinary. In normal living it's all too easy to become imprisoned by schedules. You might eat not necessarily because you're hungry, but because it's *time*. You might get up not because you've had all the rest you need, but because you'll be *late* if you don't. When you can "let the schedule be hanged," you will be giving the creative potential in you some time and space to emerge.

Aran Islands

Do you think these stones
   so painstaking piled up to the height of a man's waist
   and running like zippers across hundreds of miles
                     care
   whether you're a day ahead or behind
   in your holiday plans?

And this snail at my feet
   pulling its black and tan spiraled nautilus shell
   over a thicket of pasture grass—
   do you think it becomes
                     anxious
   if it does not make it
   to the next bed of clover by noon?

With what urgency does the persistent sea
   approach these soaring cliffs,
   waves nibbling at their base
   like a swarm of white ants
   each hour of every day for a dozen
                     millennia?

Even the spongy earth on which I sit

  seeps an assent, dampening my ambitions

  even more than my khakis;

  peat moss, they say, grows only an

                                    inch

  every seven years.

Enough just to sit, oneing in wonder. Let the schedule
be hanged.

PRACTICE 3: WORK THE EDGE OF YOUR COMFORT ZONE

Perhaps you are familiar with a parable that Jesus told about "playing it safe." The story goes that each worker was given a certain amount of money for which he was responsible. The workers who took risks and doubled what they had been given were rewarded; the one who played it conservatively was punished (Matthew 25:14–30). I have always believed this parable means God likes it when we "go for it"!

When it comes time for us to choose between a present occupation that no longer stimulates us and a cherished dream, we might be conservative and ignore the dream, blaming God for our discontent.

Or we may act as if it's God's fault that we allow work to take over our lives, that we never make it to the museum or theater, that we don't have time to grow a garden, that we never learned how to play a musical instrument.

Or we may have self-righteously tried to be sensible, rather than risking to see whether the universe would support some healthy extravagance.

But, in truth, I think our Creator has much more in mind. All we need to do is take a closer look at some of the more unusual flora and fauna in nature to get a glimpse of how wildly wonderful the whole of creation is. No playing it cautious here!

You Only Have To

You only have to crawl from your tent
in the morning and step to the water's edge
to see what looks like a zillion raindrops
but are really waterbugs playing on its surface
waiting to be breakfast for some hungry black bass;

you only have to look up and see the pre-dawn negligee
of rose-colored cloud draped alluringly
around the curvaceous crescent of the moon;

you only have to listen to the still-chanting crickets,
the wake-up call of crows and the energetic flutter
of wood thrush's wings,

to know that each day
draws your nose to the center of the rose,
to know that life comes at you like a phalanx
of yellow cabs in midtown Manhattan,

so you'd better be ready to step off the curb
and take your chances because the sun rising
over the ridge is telling you that the light
has just turned green.

This brings us to the bottom line: to explore the potential of our creativity, we have to be willing to take a risk. We have to trust our values and vision enough to step out in life. Even though we don't know where this step will take us. Even though we don't know where we will end up. Even though we are uncomfortable. Initially, every act of creativity is an act of will.

"What I have come to understand over four decades of teaching poetry," says emeritus professor of English John Savant, "is that the metaphorical 'leap' distinguishing the act of poetry from ordinary discourse has something in common with the volitional 'leap' distinguishing an act of faith from mere intellectual assent." An act of faith is not primarily an act of the mind, but one of the will.

In their book *The Art of Possibility*, Rosamund Stone Zander and Benjamin Zander suggest that many of the circumstances that block our creativity are based on a framework of assumptions that we carry with us. We all have routines and patterns that are helpful and supportive in our living. But sometimes we become immersed in familial and business cultures, built on certain shared understandings that have evolved from older beliefs and conditions that perpetuate themselves long after their usefulness has passed.

If we never question our patterns, or if we never stick our heads up out of the little boxes they represent, these patterns become prisons that prevent us from seeing the wider world of possibilities around us. Only when we choose to risk altering the patterns in our lives, when we take the risk to work the edge of our comfort zone, can we begin to tap into our full creative potential.

How willing are we to color outside the lines of the activity in which we are accomplished and secure? What would it be like to let our creative energies run free like wild horses in new pastures?

Our lives are full of creative possibilities beyond the traditional arts of music, theater, painting, dance, and writing. They range from knitting a sweater to designing a shelf, from photographing friends to planting a garden, from making cranberry bread to taking a course in storytelling. Once we have granted that we have some small measure of creativity—though by no means yet think of ourselves as artists—the next step is to project our creativity into a realm *other* than one in which we are comfortable.

For Don Quixote, it meant becoming a knight errant and roaming the world in search of adventure, to right the wrongs he encountered on his way, and to raise up the weak and those in need. But we don't have to roam the world for our adventures; what's under our feet and within our reach offers us plenty of possibilities.

For the athlete, it may mean learning to paint landscapes. For the woodworker, it may mean experimenting with new recipes in the kitchen. For the science teacher, it may mean taking voice lessons.

For the office manager, it might be to apply those organizational gifts to a community service project. For the recluse with the rich inner life, it might be to plan a party to strengthen external relationships. For a person whose office is in the home, it might be to plan a faraway trip.

Each new venture involves some measure of ego risk: "I might look clumsy or foolish." "Here I am, accomplished in my field, and I'll be starting out learning some basics." "It could be embarrassing." All that might be true. But creativity demands a certain willingness to surrender our sense of mastery.

One of the greatest obstacles to giving ourselves permission to experiment and work the edge of our comfort zone is perfectionism.

Perfectionism

It creeps into the mind
like microscopic lice,
creating a mental itch
or evoking nibbling mice.

It cracks its bullwhip
two inches from your ear,
and holds you to the task
when no one else is near.

And on the morning after
when the talk is of success,
it's a dust speck in your eye
that inclines you to regress.

"The tables were too close,"
or, "The music was too loud."
"I didn't play long enough
to satisfy the crowd."

On this infecting virus
the tables need be turned,
the bar dropped notches down
and the inner critic burned.

For if this tyrant has its way
you'll never learn to paint,
play an instrument or sing,
paralyzed by everlast complaint.

If we're honest with ourselves, most of us could offer some examples of things we'd love to do but never actually tried for fear of not meeting our own inner standards. Our long sojourn in the bleachers, when we could be on the field, is oftentimes self-imposed.

Listening to our longing involves the recognition that we do not have to be perfect. When we can care less about being perfect, we are more willing to take a risk.

In *The Artist's Way*, Julia Cameron offers another possibility for why we stay secure in our comfort zone: "One reason we are miserly with ourselves is scarcity thinking. We don't want our luck to run out. We don't want to overspend our spiritual abundance."

Hope

> *Hope perches on the pinnacle of pause,*
> *between inhalation and exhalation,*
> *releasing retention, relying on a miracle*
> *and discovering there is always more*
> *for you and for all.*
>
> *Fear stands vigilant atop a diaphragm dam*
> *built by the specter of scarcity*
> *and restricting the free flow of air*
> *from sweeping you over the falls*
> *in wild abandon into the deep pool of*
> *abundance.*

"Discovering there is always more." If we remember that our Creator is a limitless source of energy and resources, we are more apt to be willing to push beyond our comfort zone, to get beyond our fear of failure and "go for it." When we can allow ourselves to believe in the abundance of both the creative potential within us and the creative possibilities outside of us, we can find the confidence to work the edge of our comfort zone. And, as any explorer knows, the experience of life is both rich and intense on the edge.

On the Edge

We walked up the hill
through the meadow
by the light of the moon
and stepped across
the threshold
into the woods.

Right there, on the edge,
crickets' chorus
swirled around us
in vibrating waves
of sound.

But even twenty footfalls
further into the forest
and the pulsating chant
now echoed thinly
at our backs.

Life is most intensely lived
on the edge.

PRACTICE 4: SURRENDER TO THE ADVENTURE

At the outset of this book, I began with the poem "Soul Fire," posing the question of our accumulating years: "If not now, when?" and I wrote of the "surrender" required to set us free:

And the only obedience that will set you free
is surrender to the energy and fire
congealed in your gifts.

This idea of "surrender" is worth further consideration because it touches on our deeper fears of what will happen if we "let go."

Surrender

Surrender is a weakness word
in childhood games and
wrestling romps with peers.
But through the years I've come
to see that what it really does
is set you free.

I don't mean here the kind
that comes from fear and poverty;
the letting go I have in mind
requires a sense of safety and security.

While it does pry our fingers
loose from surrogate divinities,
the actual power to surrender is
only given when the heart is tender.

When the inner garden slowly grows
in readiness, the grace is given,
not as something owed, but as

a gift bestowed—almost as though
while we sleep, our hearts breathe deep
and are made ready for letting go.

When Father Bede listened to his longing and let go of his familiar life in Oxford for the unknown of India, he didn't know where it would lead him. But that's the adventure of living. When we can allow ourselves to let go of what we "know" to explore new frontiers and reframe the till-now picture of our lives, amazing things begin to unfold.

When the prison inmates in *Man of La Mancha* tried to get Cervantes to throw away his poetry, he responded, "To be a poet you need imagination, and with imagination you can have a dream."

To have a *dream* is not the same as having a *plan*. In fact, I would go so far as to say that we can only have a creative adventure when we *don't* have everything all planned out! Creativity is a marvelous balance between risk and trust. When a musician, guided by an inner inspiration, sits down and begins to plink away at the piano keys, she doesn't know exactly where it's going. When a cook gets an idea for a new combination of ingredients he's never tried before, he doesn't know what it's going to taste like, but he trusts his instinct. When an architect conceives of a new design, there are a thousand details that remain to be worked out before the dream becomes reality.

When the creative impulse moves within me in the direction of a poem, it's like stepping into a labyrinth. I don't know where it's taking me, but I trust the process to lead me to the center. And generally, "It's the Strangest Thing":

It's the strangest thing
how from the first time
an inspiration is given
some poems want to rhyme.

It's like a baby coming naturally
rather than by Caesarean section;
that's just the way the words come out—
it's not by choice or election.

Within the first two lines
it's there, for better or for worse,
like announcing "it's a boy" or "girl!"—
it's either born rhymed or blank verse.

Allowing ourselves to be led by the gut rather than the head may feel strange. If our personality type is "thinking" rather than "feeling," creative practices may "feel" illogical or counterintuitive to our normal understanding of how things operate. But that is part of their objective: to initiate a new approach to current conditions.

There is a tantalizing phrase in the Christian scriptures that has always spoken to me: "Come and see." Jesus posed this response to two of John the Baptist's followers when they came after Jesus to find out whether he was the promised one. One of Jesus's disciples, a man named Philip, responded with these same words when Nathaniel asked, "Can anything good come out of Nazareth?" (John 1:46). A woman who met Jesus by a well made the same demand of the people of her village: "Come and see" (John 4:29). And the sisters of Lazarus, when questioned by Jesus where they had buried their brother, simply said, "Come and see" (John 11:34). Every time those on the receiving end of that invitation accepted it, something life-changing happened.

When we "come and see" we open ourselves to the unpredictable. Whether the medium be rhythm, image, or diction, we resonate with the most elemental and sublime levels of consciousness, with our sense of what is truly real. Music, for example, is both wordless and pictureless, and it reaches us on a level deeper than the cognitive. Emily Dickinson testified to this resonance when she said that she recognized a "real" poem not when its argument or sympathies pleased her, but when it simply "tore my head off." It is this quality of resonance-with-the-real that led Irish poet Seamus Heaney to call the "fully realized poem" a "raid upon the inarticulate."

The idea of surrendering to something that can "tear our heads off" can be a frightening prospect. Yet opening to the wild and wonderful doesn't mean becoming wacko and weird. There is always a balance to be struck between the impulsive, from-the-heart reaction and the measured, thoughtful response.

I am reminded of another New Testament story in the Gospel of John that describes one of Jesus's resurrection appearances to his disciples (John 21). They had been out fishing all night when one of them spotted Jesus on the shore and said to the others in the boat, "It is the Lord!" Peter, the impulsive one, followed his heart, jumped into the water, and started swimming for shore. But John stayed in the boat, as if to say, "Well, let's take one thing at a time here. Get the fish in the boat, and then we'll sail for shore." A more rational approach: "We can have the net full of fish and talk to the Lord, too. Let's keep our wits about us."

There are many possible reflections on this story. Within the train of thought of this chapter, it's worth noting that, just as Jesus loved both Peter and John, we need to embrace both sides of our nature: the impulsive and the rational. Both the carefully thought out and the passionate response to the longings of our hearts have their place in the rhythm of a creative life.

Ignatius of Loyola, a sixteenth-century Spanish knight who founded the Catholic order of priests called the Jesuits, is considered by many to be the "Master of Discernment." He wrote much about his struggles to be able to recognize which of his desires came from God and which drew him away from God, which he should act on and which he should not. For many today, his "Rules for Discernment" provide a foundation for spiritual guidance. One of Ignatius's guiding principles is that careful attention to our inner desires is absolutely necessary if we want to know God's desires for our lives.

Yet, without discernment, just surrendering to inner desires may lead to some fanciful flights that end in crash landings. All of our feelings are data for discernment. It makes consummate sense to step back from desires and longings to see where they might lead, and to refrain from endorsing our initial reactions until their credentials have been checked out and validated. Once that is done to the best of our ability, however, we are called to act in confidence and, from a deep place of inner freedom, to let go and let our creativity unfold.

Letting Go

The hardest thing in living
is to receive a grace
a child, a friendship, a fulfilling work
and rejoice in it for the time
it is given
without clinging
without trying to prolong
its visitation.

The pull is so strong
to close around the feeling
the security offered
the identity given
the comfort found;
to lock it up
and possess it,

to freeze the flow
of time and events
saying "Here. Now. Forever!"

But frozen goods
break the teeth.
Better to embrace
the thawed, life-giving moment
in openhearted thanks,
carrying the gift lightly
in one's hands without grasping,
receiving it as promise and call
to live on the edge of divine desire,
allowing the inner urgent longing
to daily make the blood run
and keep the eyes open and focused,
squinting in the sun toward
the horizon of our ultimate hope.

QUESTIONS FOR REFLECTION

What do you *really* long for? Power, money, prestige, peace, joy, health, contentment? Without putting judgments on your deep desires, make a list of what you want most in the next year of your life ... in the next ten years ... before you die.

We all carry within ourselves the rational and intuitive, the masculine and feminine. Which do you think operates more strongly within yourself? Identify some examples of each in your behaviors.

Suppose that, in the interest of tapping your creative potential, you were to undertake something you'd like to try, or want to be better at, but that would be outside your comfort zone. What might that be? List two or three possibilities.

Can you identify areas of your life where you tend to engage in "scarcity thinking"? Where do you hold back from "going for it" because you're afraid your luck might run out or you'll overspend your spiritual abundance? What might it mean for you to "surrender to the adventure"?

Since all feelings are data for discernment, this means refraining from endorsing initial reactions until we have a chance to "check out their credentials." Go back to the first question and revisit your list of desires. Then step back from them for a week or so while you reflect on this question for each one: where might acting on this desire take me?

EXERCISES TO ACCESS YOUR CREATIVITY

Listen to Your Longings

Book in for a quiet weekend at a retreat center. Leave all your reading material and high-tech gadgets at home. Just spend time with yourself—walking in the woods, swinging in a hammock, sitting by a window—observing and listening to the dreams, fantasies, and deep-seated desires that surface.

Have Your Own Experience

If you're not a golfer, go to a driving range, rent a bucket of balls, and just have your own experience swinging at and (sometimes!) hitting the balls.

If you seldom get the opportunity to cook, claim the kitchen for a given time, open a recipe book, pick something you'd enjoy eating, savor the process of preparing it, and don't worry about the results.

Work the Edge of Your Comfort Zone

If you like things tidy and comfy and tend to stay behind screens in the summer time, ask friends who camp if they'd take you along next time.

Ask someone you know who has a particular skill—such as playing the harmonica or tinkering with cars—if he or she would teach you a few of the fundamentals.

Engage your insecurities around computer-related things by learning how to download music to an iPod or develop a PowerPoint presentation that you could use in your work.

Surrender to the Adventure

The next time you take a holiday trip—or just head off for a weekend—instead of plotting out carefully where you'll go and locking yourself in with advance reservations, put your bags in the car and drive in a general direction, letting the trip take you. Stop when something catches your interest and allow yourself to stay with it as long as it holds you. Move on when you could enjoy yourself more by doing something else. See how free and flexible you can be. Keep a journal of the surprising and serendipitous things that happen along the way.

I would rather be ashes than dust!
I would rather that my spark
should burn out in a brilliant blaze
than it should be stifled by dry-rot.
I would rather be a superb meteor,
every atom of me in magnificent glow,
than a sleepy and permanent planet.
The proper function of man is to live, not to exist.
I shall not waste my days in trying to prolong them.
I shall use my time.

—"CREDO," ATTRIBUTED TO JACK LONDON

SIX

Four Spiritual Gifts of Creativity

For many of us, the second half of life is a wake-up call. As we face the finiteness of the human condition, we sense a pressing need to do more that just "exist." We resonate with Jack London's fierce statement, "I would rather be ashes than dust!" We feel the heat of the smoldering embers of creativity within us. We feel the urgency of midlife and its corresponding call to recognize, accept responsibility for, and give expression to our creative fire. The impulse to create is strong, and we are ready.

This is the time to take the risk, to open to the adventure. And with the first step, the gifts of creativity begin to unfold:

- Connecting with your Creator
- Awakening more fully to life
- Unleashing the power of imagination
- Enjoying the surprise of grace

GIFT 1: CONNECTING WITH YOUR CREATOR

God-Shaped Emptiness

*There's a God-shaped emptiness
at the belly of my being,
a psychic black hole
that sends me forever wandering
like a beggar, bowl in hand,
extending my arms toward
creatures and their comforts
or whatever holds the hope
of easing the hunger.*

*Wisdom comes slowly,
building a shrine
in the homestead of the hara,
learning at every table
to put down the fork
before feeling filled,
offering the vacant space within
as a puja at the altar of awareness
so that you know that I know
some holes can't be filled.*

In the fifth century Augustine of Hippo gave witness to this "God-shaped emptiness" with his memorable line, "Our hearts are restless, O God, until they rest in Thee." We are hardwired for union with the

Divine. We were made for "come-union." The rich Christian monastic traditions of both East and West stand as living testimony to the powerful pull of this "hole in the heart" that seeks to be filled. The very essence of monasticism, according to the rule of St. Benedict, is "to truly seek God." It is this yearning for union with the Divine that draws so many people to monasteries as places of spiritual practice.

A trip to Ireland once provided me with an opportunity to visit Skellig Michael, an upthrust of rock inhabited by monks for six hundred years, going back to 588. The monks lived in "beehive" huts, perched above nearly vertical cliffs, an hour's boat ride off the coast. Today the only tangible evidence of this extraordinary monastic achievement consists of pieces of crumbling masonry, but the feeling of intense spirituality is still strong in this place.

Skellig Michael

Who were these spirit-wrestlers
 at the edge of the world,
freely choosing to live on a six-acre
 arrowhead flung upward from the sea?

Who were these men of the Absolute,
 carving from rock 2,300 wending,
winding, spiraling steps to the sky,
 each one a monument in itself?

Who were these artisans
 of the inner landscape,
building serenity, solitude, and sanctity
 into every step,

corbeling stone and beehive huts,
watertight, still standing stout
against a millennia and a half
of Atlantic tempests and gales?

Who were these denizens of desire,
seeking a vision of God in every
mood of sea and cloud, in tenuous
moss-green lichen and gannet's graceful glide?

Who were these super naturalists
whose quest for harmony of spirit
and flesh with all living things
oxidized so clean,

whose singularity of purpose
flamed so hot as to still draw pilgrims
to warm themselves by the yet-glowing embers
of their fire?

Are any still alive whose hearts so burn?

At the Tushita Meditation Centre in Dharamsala, high in the Himalayas, I took a course titled "The Graduated Path: A Synthesis of All the Buddha's Teachings." The instructors introduced our class of mostly Westerners to a world every bit as exotic as the one down below in the streets of India. Buddhism's cosmology, on first blush, feels strangely akin to Tolkein's world in *The Lord of the Rings*. It is a universe of sentient beings, arhats, bodhicittas, bodhisattvas, magical emanations, karmic imprints, nirvana, and hungry ghosts.

But beyond the spirit-world of Buddhism and the pantheon of Hindu deities, something else came through in my studies in India. As Beatrice Bruteau observes in her book *What We Can Learn from the East*, the first thing we can discover is that religion is foremost a matter of direct experience. The emphasis is not on believing or endorsing propositions of faith or on holding correct opinions, but on living contact with the Absolute.

Direct spiritual experience shifts our sense of who and what we are, what is going on, what "good" is, and what we should do about it. Direct spiritual experience gives us the conviction that we are natural residents of the realm of the Beyond and the Whole, that we are loved and created to love, that it is our nature to be creative. From such direct experience, great quantities of energy are released in the world.

If you've ever traveled to India perhaps you'll understand when I say that there is a pervasive sense of the Sacred in the air. For Hindus, God is an immanent presence: in your breath, your mind, the animals, the flowers—everywhere! Wherever you go and whatever you do, God is there. For the typical Hindu villager every action has a sacred significance: Bathing is a sacred rite. Water comes from heaven. Food is a gift from God. Marriage is a sacred bond. There are eleven different rites to consecrate a child—before birth, after birth, and so on. The *namaste* gesture, a slight bow in the direction of another with hands folded, recognizes God in every human heart. There is an underlying longing to experience God, a desire to deal more directly with things of the heart and spirit.

This is precisely the contribution that artistic pursuits make: creative expression links us in a moment of recognition, of communion with our Creator, and opens us up to new realms of intimacy with the Divine.

In her book *Every Changing Shape: Mystical Experience and the Making of Poems*, English poet Elizabeth Jennings proposes that mystical experience and poetry-making—indeed, all music and art—spring from the same creative source: the very center of the human soul that knows direct contact with God. I would go one step further and pose that the very writing of exalted poetry or prose or music is *itself* a kind of contact with God because all art is a participation in the eternal act of creation.

In the way creativity reaches out and grabs us by the heart at unexpected times, it reaffirms that the Holy will meet us when it chooses, not just when we choose. The meeting place may be in a park or concert hall or mountaintop, just as well as in a church.

When we live in the absence of the Sacred, we are not yet our fullest selves. Our innate capacity for intimate communion with God has yet to open its petals to reveal the full splendor of our humanity, the creature in conscious relationship with the Creator, the mortal with the Immortal. But even to be aware of God's absence is to long for God's presence—and not only for God's presence but also for our true life, in the sense of what is deepest and best in us. Both absence and presence have their effect, but the ultimate power belongs to presence. It is this longing for presence that stirs the smoldering embers of creativity within us.

Each time we pick up a pen to begin writing what may become a poem, each time we touch a key or pluck a string to start what may become a song, each time we take that first step of what may become a dance, we are doing what we were made for: each creative action deepens our communion with our Creator.

GIFT 2: AWAKENING MORE FULLY TO LIFE

On the occasion of the one-hundredth anniversary of the laying of the foundation stone of the National Cathedral in Washington, D. C., the Litany of Remembrance and Thanksgiving began with this prayer:

God spoke, and the material world came into being. God called forth creation, blessed it, and declared it good. Day by day, we see everywhere the glory of creation: in trees, water, and the works of human hands.... We offer these symbols as a reminder of the divine grace that comes to us through the material of our daily lives.

The varying material elements used in the building of the cathedral were then brought forward in procession to the altar, with an individual prayer of thanksgiving offered for each one in turn—stone, iron, wood, needlework, glass, flowers, leaves, and all growing things that "adorn this house of prayer." Divine grace continues to come to us through these elements of creation. They are, in fact, the very places where we keep alive and active our creativity connection with the Creator.

The Qur'an asserts that the presence of the Holy is supremely accessible, "nearer than our own jugular vein." For those who have eyes to see, presence manifests in the little world within our reach and under our feet. It grows up like crabgrass in the sidewalk cracks. We have only to open our eyes to awaken to a world that, in the words of Gerard Manley Hopkins, is "charged with the grandeur of God.... There lives the dearest freshness deep down things / Because the Holy Ghost over the bent / world broods with warm breast and with ah! bright / wings."

Most people of faith think of their tradition's holy writ when they hear the word *revelation*, but there is another locus of God's self-revelation, and that is the created world. The transparency of nature to God became something of an article of faith for the English romantic poets, such as Wordsworth and Coleridge. The medium of their poetry and the message of nature were always intimately connected. They felt that nature's goal of bringing us more fully to life made it as rich a language for spirituality as scripture.

Perhaps more than any other realm, nature's "theater of the seasons" is an expression of God's astonishing creativity. Each season speaks its own word of instruction for living abundantly; each season teaches us to see life afresh. In many respects, this is the quintessential essence of creativity: to see the world, brimming with possibilities, from a new perspective.

AUTUMN

How many of us know people for whom fall is their favorite season? Is it simply because of the colors? Or could it be that nature's way of dying speaks to us on a spiritual level of how we want to live: with energy and luminous expression, rejoicing in diversity and bursts of extravagance?

O But to Live as Nature Dies!

O but to live as nature dies—
with luminous expression
and phosphorescent bursts of being!

To flow with the energy of one's calling
like the glaciers of gold and orange
that swirl down mountain valleys.

To warm oneself with the heat of love
like the cone-shaped evergreen chimneys
surround themselves with the burning coals of molten
  maples.

To exude a joy in living
like a grove of yellow aspen exploding
in a mushrooming cloud of radiant light.

To rejoice in the diversity of peoples and cultures
as in the painter's palette of colors
generously splotched on the hillsides.

O but to live as nature dies——
with such liberality of being to soften the end
as autumn does with winter.

WINTER

Although many "snow birds" fly south for the winter to escape the cold and ice, snow too speaks to us of eternal things. Words about snow become instruments for speaking about the mystery of grace through symbol and metaphor.

Snow Mass

Daily it falls like fluffy, feathered fleece,
spiraling down in absolution for our spirit's sweet release,
soothing souls with wonder, tranquility, and peace.

It floats softly on the air like crystalline-shaped grace,
gently covering every bush and tree with a mantel of
*   white lace,*
enfolding all that lives in its delicate embrace.

Dropped silently from the clouds like myriad points of light,
it gathers to a greatness in a billion beams all rolled up tight,
faintly glowing in the darkness and illumining the night.

Then, appearing in the morning like manna heaven-sent,
the heart leaps up in wonder, and knees to earth are bent,
turning us into children with all "the days 'til Christmas"
    spent.

To break the hush of nature, no animal risks defiance;
here the cloister of winter stillness reigns in holy
    self-reliance
and subtly makes it known that God's favored tongue is
    silence.

Silent music stirs the soul as all creatures bow and pass,
leaving tracks of glory, inciting marvel in the crass;
all creation vests in white for a glorious snow Mass.

SPRING

Each season speaks a living word to us, but spring, especially, sings of life.

Life Reigns!

The frigid compress of winter
came in layers of ice
around the turn of the year,
sheets of freezing rain
that fell for days
and chilled one's soul,

laying down a burden of crystal death,
forcing trees to bow low
in painful compliance
and finally crack
like brittle bones,
pinning bushes to the ground
with a vice-like grip
of cold-blooded strangulation.

Comes the longed-for warmth of Spring:
an April morning
sitting in the garden
surrounded by fallen limbs
and entire uprooted trees,
surveying a hillside of brush
with spines forever crushed.
A cardinal fills the air
with birdsong
from a surviving branch above
and a robin dances amidst
an astonishment of crocus
pushing up prodigiously
through the chaotic cover
of twigs and leaves——
sheaves of green
piercing the thawing earth
and opening delicate petals
of blue rebirth

as once again
the message bursts forth
from the tomb of death:
Life reigns!

SUMMER

In Celtic spirituality, Nature is God's "big book" of revelation and the Bible is the "little book." Once we learn to open the pages of the big book, the "living words" are everywhere to be read.

Summer

It can happen in any season
but the heart has a better chance
of opening to life in summer
when the clothes come off
and we're down to hairy legs and halter tops.

That expansive throw-back-your-head-and-laugh
response to life in the face of all that still sits
in the sink or on the desk
is more effectively coaxed from the heart
in the season of boat rides and backyard barbeques.

The deep-belly conviction that the world
will be kind to us floats up more easily

in the longer, warmer light of summer,
in the street musician's free concert by the curb
and in exploding fireworks against a starry sky.

The discovery of the leisurely, relaxed step
and the comfort of friendly words with neighbors
comes with turning over garden dirt,
watering the flowers and tomatoes,
sharing apples, cucumbers, and corn on the cob.

It could happen in November or December,
but the opening of the heart to life
is given broader berth amidst Rocky Road and sticky skin
with the music floating out the window
and the children catching fireflies in the yard.

GIFT 3: UNLEASHING THE POWER OF IMAGINATION

Consider for a moment the power of imagination and memory. For the greater part of every day, our brains are processing information in linear fashion. But when we listen to a piece of music, thousands of neurons in the brain that would otherwise have lain dormant are stimulated. The music evokes memories, places, people, experiences. It engages our emotions and takes us back to an outdoor concert under the stars or a quiet evening with a friend in front of a fireplace.

Depth psychologist James Hillman says that the creative process begins when powerful experiences drive us inward. In these depths, our psyches begin to grope for metaphors to capture the experience: "It is like this or like that ..." The artistic act, then, becomes a vehicle by which we can express our encounter with ultimate reality. Creative artistic expression—the sculptor's figures, the weaver's tapestry, the painter's fresco—conveys our deepest experiences of being lost, loved, wounded, healed. They make the spiritual real.

The arts in general—and, for me, poetry in particular—have the power to bring us face to face with our own experience in ways we had not yet recognized. They offer an opportunity to discourse about the hidden, invisible realities of the spiritual life. I like the description of a poem that L. William Countryman offers in his book *The Poetic Imagination*: "a little world built to convey something of the larger world, something rooted in experience." His words capture the ability of creative expression to open us to something bigger, brighter, beyond us.

When something is incarnated in words or color or shape or sound, not only does the creator experience life in a new way, with greater depth or clarity or feeling, but the receiver also experiences a larger world through new eyes and ears, through new taste and touch. And in the process both come to a fuller awareness of life, a richer understanding of meaning, and a renewed sense of being more fully awake to life.

When we encounter someone's creative expression, the effect on us is similar to that of hearing a good story: it lifts us out of our matrix and lets us experience the world through another pair of eyes. Once we have seen things from a different perspective, the world may never be the same for us again. For example, poetry invites readers to enter into an imaginative process similar to that of the writer's. Poems take us within ourselves, to the memories we carry, to places where we feel centered and renewed; they also take us outside of ourselves, to people who enliven us and lead us to a fuller life. The poet's images also have the power to lead us to our own images—for writing poems, for painting pictures, for sculpting with clay. Through our creative response, we, too, can give our wider and deeper self a voice.

The English poet Samuel David Coleridge regarded religion as "the poetry of humankind," in that both religion and poetry prevent us from remaining in our own narrow sphere of action, our own individual circumstances. They bid us, while we are sitting in the shadows at our little fire, struggling with darkness, to announce the light that is common to all.

Coleridge might have said the same of other forms of art as well, for what a poem does—shine a light on a moment of intensity—is also what the artist seeks to do with paint or the sculptor with chisel and stone. Along the way, the literal image gives way to a metaphor that invites us to the larger meaning.

Today we have a renewed respect for the power of the human imagination to capture realities that can be expressed in no other way. In this century, our appreciation of poetic imagery has been enhanced by Carl Jung's conclusion that symbolic language is the first language of the psyche. Yet perhaps no one better exemplifies the power of poetry to go beyond ordinary speech, to articulate the ineffable, than the sixteenth-century Spanish mystic John of the Cross. John wrote poetry as his first expression of experiencing God. His poetic language addresses us at levels of our being where we are simply mute, or can only stammer. His images hint at hungers and nourishments that we recognize but cannot express.

His most powerful poems—"The Dark Night," "The Spiritual Canticle," and "The Living Flame of Love"—lay rather neglected for three centuries while writers gave priority to his prose commentary on the poems. John was way ahead of us in recognizing imagination as a power of the soul. In fact, he esteemed it so highly as to call it the "gate and entry" to the soul.

Our work, our challenge—especially in midlife—is to maintain the hinges on this gate and "oil" it, lest it become creaky and hard to open. When we feed our imaginations with what ennobles and inspires— with music, art, dance, great literature, and stories on the big screen—we draw near to the very wellspring of life. It is a powerful place—even a dangerous undertaking. It has to be, in order to move people, to touch them in their secret places. In art, we are, in effect, seeing someone else's secrets—or exposing our own. In creativity, we touch the very fire in the soul. We are tapping into one of the most elemental powers in the universe—the raw energy of creation.

GIFT 4: ENJOYING THE SURPRISE OF GRACE

In *The Poetic Imagination*, L. William Countryman posits that the English Anglican poetic tradition has a particular center that qualifies it to be thought of as a spiritual tradition: that center is surprise. The English poets are interested in the ways that the Divine surprises us, changes our minds, brings about conversion. They return again and again to the discovery and rediscovery of grace, the unpredictable, unfathomable, and, indeed, humanly impossible moment of recognizing and assenting to God's goodness. "Sometimes," writes Countryman, "this takes the form of a kind of mystical self-transcendence, but not always. Most of the time it takes the simpler form of a somewhat embarrassed encounter with delight that casts all of life in a new light."

This is the supreme gift of creativity: the experience of a surprising encounter with light, with grace. St. Augustine, the great thinker whose complete surrender to God is expressed in his immortal conversion story told in Book VIII of the *Confessions*, described how, through an act of introspection, he experienced a mystical transformation, a vision or touch, which revealed to him that God is light, a pure spiritual being.

The groundbreaking physicist Albert Einstein once said, "If something is in me which can be called religious, then it is the unbounded admiration for the structure of the world so far as our science can reveal it."

Art critic Sister Wendy Beckett said in an interview, "So many people live in a prison of daily life with no one to tell them to look out or look up. If you don't know about God, art is the only thing that can set you free. It satisfies and challenges the human spirit to accept a deeper reality."

To live creatively opens us to grace. When we open ourselves to the adventure of building, gardening, cooking, composing, crafting—of living itself—the Sacred breaks upon us with all the suddenness of a summer cloudburst. These are the experiences spiritual traditions call "mystical." Words cannot capture them, and neither human will nor spiritual practice can force them. When they come upon us as gift, the most we can do is to respond with borrowed metaphors, such as in this poem "Like a Gutted Deer," and fling them in the direction of the ineffable.

> *You left me lying today on the forest floor*
> *like a gutted deer, feebly rustling*
> *the pine needles with spasmic hooves.*
> *It all began when I lost my direction*
> *watching the tufts of fleece crawl across*
> *the sky like lobsters and crabs, and then*
> *started to dance with the lasers of light,*
> *tracing my trail through the trees*
> *until, dizzy with laughing, I fell*
> *among the pinecones and waited for*
> *you to come with your merry eyes and*
> *your skinning knife between your teeth*
> *to open me up so that I could see*
> *the soft smile on your face when*
> *from my belly there came forth*
> *only music and stars.*

In the second half of life, as we take the time to reflect on our life stories, we become more aware that we live by grace. We look back and recognize that the visitation of the Divine has always come with an element of surprise—a Mysterious Reality, to borrow the seventeenth-century poet George Herbert's words, that arrives without warning, working its transformations on us in ways that we could not have foreseen.

The Mystery we call God, the flash of radiance, the surprise of grace, is not something we can plan, predict, coerce, or demand. It is not something we can produce by sheer dint of our own efforts. It is a gift. It can burst in on us with the sound of one note; it can amaze us in the brush of one color; it can stagger us in the glimpse of one fluid movement. It can pop up before us as unexpectedly as a loon in a lake on an early morning swim:

I Heard Your Laughter

This morning, with every cell singing,
I cut a surgical opening in the skin of the lake,
and when I came up for air,
there you were, appearing as an elegant loon
in your black and white tuxedo, floating,
preening your feathers as if to say,
"Where have you been?"

I glided in close, hardly breathing,
when suddenly you disappeared from sight
and oh! How I wanted to follow you
to that dark and mysterious depth
whose air I cannot yet breathe!
Then I turned in the water and saw
your silhouette against the fiery sphere
and heard your laughter rising upon the wind.

The moment of creative inspiration has deep resonance with what might be called "the sacred moment," in which we feel the presence of the Divine, sense the mystery, and struggle to articulate it. These moments of connection with the Holy are not given to us in a constant way day in and day out. We are surprised by grace, then we return to a rather less exalted state, or perhaps even plunge into an experience of absence. The surprise of grace does not suddenly make all of human life sweetness and light, but it does lead us to a closer examination of the marvelous richness of Mystery's presence amid the limitations of human life. When something inside of us has been touched by the Sacred, we are changed and will never be the same again.

Footprints in the Sand

You stole into camp last night like an argonaut,
like David into the camp of Saul,
placing a spear in the ground by my head,
holding me captive by the south wind's warm caresses,
tenderly towseling my hair with your fingers,
breezily feathering my body, leaving me trembling,
leaving me exhausted at morning's light,
leaving my heart bounding like a child within me
when I sat up and saw your footprints in the sand.

Let me tell you a story of being surprised by grace. I was on a visit to men's and women's Orthodox monasteries in Romania. The women's monastery that I was visiting at the time, Varatec, was organized like no other monastery I had ever seen. Varatec is basically a village in the hill country, and all the inhabitants are Sisters in the monastery, with the exception of a few hired hands who help with the farmwork. There are 170 houses in the village, some central meeting halls, and three churches. The 450 Sisters in the monastic village live by twos, threes, and fours in the houses. In this way they have the benefit of a large community for work on the farm and in their other workshops, and at the same time they have the benefit of an intimate community relationship in their own homes.

The Abbess, Maica Nazaria, gave me a tour of the monastery workshops, and as we passed through them I exclaimed about the tapestries they were making, the painted eggs in preparation for Easter, the icons. A few days later, when the time came for me to depart, I was putting my things into my small carrying case when there was a knock on the door. When I opened it, there stood Maica Nazaria with her arms full of gifts—small tapestries, eggs, and icons for which I had expressed admiration during the tour of the workshops.

"I believe you liked these," she said simply. I was stupefied and didn't know what to say.

"I am very touched by your kindness," I stammered. "But, Maica, I couldn't accept these! As you see, there is no room in my bag where I could even put them."

She said a few words that I did not understand to Sister Josephina, who was standing nearby, and within a few minutes, Sister Josephina came back with a suitcase. They were not only smothering me with gifts but also providing a suitcase in which to carry them home!

We went then to the nearby church for the singing of the Office. Maica Nazaria explained to the Sisters that I would have to leave in the middle of the service to catch the train back to Bucharest. When the time came, I venerated the icons and, in a spontaneous gesture from the heart, turned and bowed to the choir on the right side of the chapel (they stood and bowed back), then did the same to the choir on the left side (they stood and bowed back), and finally turned to the choir in the loft at the back. They came to the edge of the loft and returned my bow. That was our way of saying "*la revedere*" ("until we see one another again").

Maica Nazaria ushered me out with tears in my eyes and put me in her car along with her driver, Sister Haritina, to accompany me to the train station. They waited with me until the train came, got onto the train with me to make sure that I got to my seat all right, explained to the people in my cabin that I was from Canada and spoke English and French but not Romanian, and asked them to assist me should I need help with anything. Then Maica Nazaria opened her bag and lifted out a package of food copious enough to last for three days. And Sister Haritina, who had gone back to the car, suddenly reappeared with a bouquet of fresh flowers from their garden, apparently stowed in the trunk.

I thought I knew what graciousness and hospitality were, but I had been surprised by grace.

When we are overtaken by grace—whether as recipients of an astonishing hospitality or of an inspirationally creative idea—not only is the gift a surprise, but so is the rare moment when we find in ourselves the grace to acknowledge and accept it. Poet George Herbert expressed this profound truth in his poem "Love (III)":

> *Love bade me welcome; yet my soul drew back,*
> * Guilty of dust and sin.*
> *But quick-ey'd Love, observing me grow slack*
> * From my first entrance in,*
> *Drew nearer to me, sweetly questioning,*
> * If I lacked anything.*
>
> *A guest, I answer'd, worthy to be here;*
> * Love said, You shall be he.*
> *I the unkind, ungrateful? Ah my dear,*
> * I cannot look on thee.*

Love took my hand, and smiling did reply,
  Who made the eyes but I?

Truth Lord, but I have marr'd them: let my shame
  Go where it doth deserve.
And know you not, says Love, who bore the blame?
  My dear, then I will serve.
You must sit down, says Love, and taste my meat:
  So I did sit and eat.

This poem is a powerful image of our human response to God's love, to God's insistent return to us, appealing, inviting, welcoming—and also of our bewilderment at being brought to the table of God's abundance and given a share in God's creativity. Despite the loving welcome, we may want to avoid it, to hang on to the identity of an unworthy outsider, rather than become a welcome guest. Yet the surprise that we are welcome is trumped by an even greater surprise: thanks to grace, we become free to accept the welcome, to "sit and eat."

The poem's final line captures the core of the midlife challenge: to accept the invitation to the feast of creativity.

To recognize both the gift and the responsibility of creativity is to receive all the gifts that have been set before you on the table.

To surrender to the energy congealed in your gifts is to fan the coals of your creativity into flame.

To surrender to the fire in your soul is to say: "So I did sit and eat."

QUESTIONS FOR REFLECTION

Have you ever felt a "God-shaped emptiness" in your life? What seemed to fill it?

In what season of the year do you feel most alive? Why do you think this is so? What feelings or desires does this season awaken in you?

What kinds of experiences feed your imagination? When was the last time you sought out such an experience?

What would you consider some of the sacred moments of your life?

Think of some surprises in your life that have brought you both a gift and a responsibility.

EXERCISES TO ACCESS YOUR CREATIVITY

Connecting with Your Creator

Spend some time looking at Human Anatomy Online at www.innerbody.com/htm/body.html.

Watch the BBC documentary series *Planet Earth*.

Look for the Sacred in all things today, even in the most mundane activities. Examine your food. Watch the water droplets as you shower. Marvel at the process of growth and renewal taking place in nature. Listen intently to the sounds around you.

Awakening More Fully to Life

Seek out opportunities to play with children.

Serve in a soup kitchen and become familiar with the creativity of street people to find food, clothing, and shelter.

Ask yourself regularly before going to bed at night, "Where did I experience awe today?"

Unleashing the Power of Imagination

See whether you can find some recordings of music that were popular during the decade from your fifteenth to your twenty-fifth year. Sit down and give yourself over fully to listening. Jot down the scenes that come up in your imagination and memory.

Open to one of your favorite stories in a book that you consider sacred. After reading it, place yourself in the scene by identifying with one of the characters in the story. Close your eyes and smell the odors, hear the noises, see the others. Become an active participant in the scene as events unfold in your mind's eye. Be attentive to whether and where your heart is moved.

Go see a movie that reflects state-of-the-art animation.

Select a medium such as paint, words, or movement and use it for fifteen minutes to tell a story.

Enjoying the Surprise of Grace

Recall an occasion in which you were "surprised by grace." Look for an opportunity to share it with someone close to you.

Keep a journal over the next month and write down any occasion in which you feel overtaken by grace.

Conclusion
"Get Busy Living or Get Busy Dying"

The gift of grace—and the way it takes us by surprise and sets us free—is superbly captured in a scene from the film *The Shawshank Redemption*. Andy Dufresne, a young bank vice-president, is questionably convicted of murdering his wife and her lover. He is sent to Shawshank prison for a life sentence. There he gets appointed to work in the prison's paltry library, and he begins a letter-writing campaign to the state government for more books and audiovisual materials. Six years later, crates of reading and listening material finally arrive. Unpacking them, Andy comes upon an album of the Mozart opera *The Marriage of Figaro* and puts on the duet "Sull'aria." Deeply touched by the sounds he hears coming out of the speaker, Andy brings the prison microphone over to the record player and turns it on, sending the music throughout the whole prison.

Men in the infirmary, languishing in bed, get up and go to the windows. Those in the prison yard, both prisoners and guards, stop their work and turn, looking up at the speakers, spellbound. While we watch this scene unfold, one of the inmates, Red, shares his memory of the event and says in a voice-over narrative:

> To this day, I have no idea what those two Italian ladies were singing about. Truth is, I don't want to know. Some things are best

left unsaid. I like to think they were singing about something so beautiful it can't be expressed in words, and makes your heart ache. I tell you, those voices *soared*, higher and farther than anybody in a great place dares to dream. It was like some beautiful bird flopped into our drab little cage and made those walls dissolve away. And for the briefest of moments, every last man in Shawshank prison felt free.

It was a spiritual moment.

At the end of the film, both Andy and Red are out of prison. Andy writes a note to Red, inviting him to join him in Mexico, where he now has a little place by the sea, telling him to "get busy living, or get busy dying."

That is the invitation of the inner creative spirit: you are created to create. The creative potential within you is one of the things that makes you "in the image and likeness of God." Whether your medium be music, watercolors, clay, gardening, woodworking, cooking, dance, or voice, the Creator has gifted you with creativity. Your gift in return is to use it.

As Andy said to Red, "Get busy living, or get busy dying."

Sunset

Go.
Put down the book.
Open the door and step outside.
This sunset will last only a few moments.
In these clouds your life and whole world are reflected.
This golden fleece curled about the mountain
asks you to open your soul
to be all here
now.

Soon
this radiant glow
like all we love will be pulled beyond
our tenacious grasping in the flow of time.
The only answer is to open your heart to it fully,
to let your eyes fill with tears of tenderness
at the dizzying, knee-buckling beauty
delivered all unordered for your
awakening.

Suggestions for Further Reading

Allegretti, Joseph G. *Loving Your Job, Finding Your Passion: Work and the Spiritual Life*. Mahwah, NJ: Paulist Press, 2000.

Arrien, Angeles. *The Second Half of Life*. Boulder, CO: Sounds True, 2005.

Barry, William A., S.J. *Allowing the Creator to Deal with the Creature: An Approach to the Spiritual Exercises of Ignatius of Loyola*. Mahwah, NJ: Paulist Press, 1994.

Bruteau, Beatrice. *What We Can Learn from the East*. New York: Crossroads, 1994.

Cameron, Julia. *The Artist's Way: A Spiritual Path to Higher Creativity*. New York: Jeremy P. Tarcher/Putnam, 1992.

Countryman, L. William. *The Poetic Imagination: An Anglican Spiritual Tradition*. Maryknoll, NY: Orbis, 2000.

Didyk, Laura. "Off the Mat: Living the Illuminated Life." *Kripalu Online*, March 1, 2007.

du Boulay, Shirley. "Father Bede's Breakthrough." *The Tablet*, September 12, 1998.

Einstein, Albert. In *Albert Einstein, The Human Side: New Glimpses from His Archives*. Edited by Banesh Hoffman and Helen Dukas. Princeton, NJ: Princeton University Press, 1981.

Herbert, George. *The Country Parson, The Temple*. Edited by John N. Wall Jr. New York: Paulist Press, 1981.

Hillman, James. *Re-Visioning Psychology*. New York: Harper and Row, 1975.

Jennings, Elizabeth. *Every Changing Shape: Mystical Experience and the Making of Poems*. Manchester, England: Carcanet Press, 1961/1996.

Levitin, Daniel. Cited in Clive Thompson, "Music of the Hemispheres." *The New York Times*, December 31, 2006, Arts & Leisure.

London, Jack. "Credo." Jack London's literary executor, Irving Shepard, quoted this "Jack London Credo" in an introduction to a 1956 collection of Jack London stories, though Shepard did not cite a source. These words also appeared in a story in the *San Francisco Bulletin*, December 2, 1916, by journalist Ernest J. Hopkins, who visited London's ranch just weeks before London's death.

Nelson, Gertrud Mueller. *To Dance with God*. Mahwah, NJ: Paulist Press, 1986.

O'Connor, Peter. *Understanding Jung, Understanding Yourself*. Mahwah, NJ: Paulist Press, 1985.

Richards, M. C. *Centering in Pottery, Poetry, and the Person*. Middletown, CT: Wesleyan University Press, 1962, 1989.

Ryan, Thomas. *Four Steps to Spiritual Freedom*. Mahwah, NJ: Paulist Press, 2003.

———. *The Sacred Art of Fasting: Preparing to Practice*. Woodstock, VT: SkyLight Paths Publishing, 2005.

———. *Yoga Prayer*. (DVD). Boulder, CO: Sounds True, 2004.

Savant, John. "Follow That Metaphor: What Faith, Jazz, & Poetry Have in Common." *Commonweal*, November 18, 2005.

Underhill, Evelyn. *Practical Mysticism*. Columbus, OH: Ariel Press, 1957.

Vaughan-Lee, Llewellyn. "Love and Longing: The Feminine Mysteries of Love." Inverness, CA: The Golden Sufi Center, 1999.

Wakefield, Dan. *Releasing the Creative Spirit: Unleash the Creativity in Your Life*. Woodstock, VT: SkyLight Paths Publishing, 2001.

Whyte, David. "Images of Fire: Poetry and Personal Passion." *Creation Spirituality*, March/April 1992.
Authors Note: See David Whyte's website for futher information on his books and recordings: davidwhyte.bigmindcatalyst.com

Williamson, Marianne. *A Return to Love*. New York: HarperCollins, 1992.

Zander, Rosamund Stone, and Benjamin Zander. *The Art of Possibility: Transforming Professional and Personal Life*. New York: Penguin Books, 2002.

Acknowledgments

I am grateful to Emily Wichland, vice-president of editorial and production at SkyLight Paths, for her enthusiastic response to this manuscript even in its penultimate form, as well as to editors Maura Shaw and Jon Sweeney, and to friend Cindy Sollecito, each of whom provided helpful comments at earlier stages along the way.

I also want to express appreciation to friends and participants in various programs and retreats over the years for their encouragement to "go public" with my poetry.

During the eight-year span in which the manuscript for this book slowly took form, I authored or coauthored five other books. This one has been like the child in a large family who requires special attention, greater patience, and more love. It is without a doubt the most personal book I have ever written; to share your poetry is also to share the secrets of your soul. That, too, is an acknowledgment.

Finally, I want to lay a wreath of flowers at the feet of my gifted and exacting editor, Marcia Broucek, who, like an able and experienced scout, kept pointing the way forward, inspiring confidence and providing encouragement toward the promised land of publication.

To all of you, my heartfelt thanks.

Global Spiritual Perspectives

Spiritual Perspectives on America's Role as Superpower
by the Editors at SkyLight Paths
Are we the world's good neighbor or a global bully? From a spiritual perspective, what are America's responsibilities as the only remaining superpower? Contributors:
Dr. Beatrice Bruteau • Dr. Joan Brown Campbell • Tony Campolo • Rev. Forrest Church • Lama Surya Das • Matthew Fox • Kabir Helminski • Thich Nhat Hanh • Eboo Patel • Abbot M. Basil Pennington, ocso • Dennis Prager • Rosemary Radford Ruether • Wayne Teasdale • Rev. William McD. Tully • Rabbi Arthur Waskow • John Wilson
5½ x 8½, 256 pp, Quality PB, 978-1-893361-81-2 **$16.95**

Spiritual Perspectives on Globalization, 2nd Edition
Making Sense of Economic and Cultural Upheaval
by Ira Rifkin; Foreword by Dr. David Little, Harvard Divinity School
What is globalization? Surveys the religious landscape. Includes a new Discussion Guide designed for group use.
5½ x 8½, 256 pp, Quality PB, 978-1-59473-045-0 **$16.99**

Hinduism / Vedanta

The Four Yogas
A Guide to the Spiritual Paths of Action, Devotion, Meditation and Knowledge
by Swami Adiswarananda
6 x 9, 320 pp, Quality PB, 978-1-59473-223-2 **$19.99**; HC, 978-1-59473-143-3 **$29.99**

Meditation & Its Practices
A Definitive Guide to Techniques and Traditions of Meditation in Yoga and Vedanta
by Swami Adiswarananda 6 x 9, 504 pp, Quality PB, 978-1-59473-105-1 **$24.99**

The Spiritual Quest and the Way of Yoga: The Goal, the Journey and the Milestones
by Swami Adiswarananda 6 x 9, 288 pp, HC, 978-1-59473-113-6 **$29.99**

Sri Ramakrishna, the Face of Silence
by Swami Nikhilananda and Dhan Gopal Mukerji
Edited with an Introduction by Swami Adiswarananda; Foreword by Dhan Gopal Mukerji II
Classic biographies present the life and thought of Sri Ramakrishna.
6 x 9, 352 pp, HC, 978-1-59473-115-0 **$29.99**

Sri Sarada Devi, The Holy Mother: Her Teachings and Conversations
Translated with Notes by Swami Nikhilananda; Edited with an Introduction by Swami Adiswarananda
6 x 9, 288 pp, HC, 978-1-59473-070-2 **$29.99**

The Vedanta Way to Peace and Happiness *by Swami Adiswarananda*
6 x 9, 240 pp, Quality PB, 978-1-59473-180-8 **$18.99**

Vivekananda, World Teacher: His Teachings on the Spiritual Unity of Humankind
Edited and with an Introduction by Swami Adiswarananda
6 x 9, 272 pp, Quality PB, 978-1-59473-210-2 **$21.99**

Sikhism

The First Sikh Spiritual Master
Timeless Wisdom from the Life and Teachings of Guru Nanak *by Harish Dhillon*
Tells the story of a unique spiritual leader who showed a gentle, peaceful path to God-realization while highlighting Guru Nanak's quest for tolerance and compassion. 6 x 9, 192 pp, Quality PB, 978-1-59473-209-6 **$16.99**

Or phone, fax, mail or e-mail to: SKYLIGHT PATHS Publishing
Sunset Farm Offices, Route 4 • P.O. Box 237 • Woodstock, Vermont 05091
Tel: (802) 457-4000 • Fax: (802) 457-4004 • www.skylightpaths.com
Credit card orders: (800) 962-4544 (8:30AM–5:30PM ET Monday–Friday)
Generous discounts on quantity orders. SATISFACTION GUARANTEED. Prices subject to change.

Spiritual Poetry—The Mystic Poets

Experience these mystic poets as you never have before. Each beautiful, compact book includes: a brief introduction to the poet's time and place; a summary of the major themes of the poet's mysticism and religious tradition; essential selections from the poet's most important works; and an appreciative preface by a contemporary spiritual writer.

Hafiz
The Mystic Poets
Preface by Ibrahim Gamard
Hafiz is known throughout the world as Persia's greatest poet, with sales of his poems in Iran today only surpassed by those of the Qur'an itself. His probing and joyful verse speaks to people from all backgrounds who long to taste and feel divine love and experience harmony with all living things.
5 x 7¼, 144 pp, HC, 978-1-59473-009-2 **$16.99**

Hopkins
The Mystic Poets
Preface by Rev. Thomas Ryan, CSP
Gerard Manley Hopkins, Christian mystical poet, is beloved for his use of fresh language and startling metaphors to describe the world around him. Although his verse is lovely, beneath the surface lies a searching soul, wrestling with and yearning for God.
5 x 7¼, 112 pp, HC, 978-1-59473-010-8 **$16.99**

Tagore
The Mystic Poets
Preface by Swami Adiswarananda
Rabindranath Tagore is often considered the "Shakespeare" of modern India. A great mystic, Tagore was the teacher of W. B. Yeats and Robert Frost, the close friend of Albert Einstein and Mahatma Gandhi, and the winner of the Nobel Prize for Literature. This beautiful sampling of Tagore's two most important works, *The Gardener* and *Gitanjali*, offers a glimpse into his spiritual vision that has inspired people around the world.
5 x 7¼, 144 pp, HC, 978-1-59473-008-5 **$16.99**

Whitman
The Mystic Poets
Preface by Gary David Comstock
Walt Whitman was the most innovative and influential poet of the nineteenth century. This beautiful sampling of Whitman's most important poetry from *Leaves of Grass,* and selections from his prose writings, offers a glimpse into the spiritual side of his most radical themes—love for country, love for others, and love of Self.
5 x 7¼, 192 pp, HC, 978-1-59473-041-2 **$16.99**

Journeys of Simplicity
Traveling Light with Thomas Merton, Bashō, Edward Abbey, Annie Dillard & Others
Invites you to consider a more graceful way of traveling through life. Use the included journal pages (in PB only) to help you get started on your own spiritual journey.

Ed. by Philip Harnden
5 x 7¼, 144 pp, Quality PB, 978-1-59473-181-5 **$12.99**
128 pp, HC, 978-1-893361-76-8 **$16.95**

Prayer / Meditation

Sacred Attention: A Spiritual Practice for Finding God in the Moment
by Margaret D. McGee
Framed on the Christian liturgical year, this inspiring guide explores ways to develop a practice of attention as a means of talking—and listening—to God.
6 x 9, 144 pp, HC, 978-1-59473-232-4 **$19.99**

Women Pray: Voices through the Ages, from Many Faiths, Cultures and Traditions
Edited and with Introductions by Monica Furlong
5 x 7¼, 256 pp, Quality PB, 978-1-59473-071-9 **$15.99**

Women of Color Pray: Voices of Strength, Faith, Healing,
Hope and Courage   *Edited and with Introductions by Christal M. Jackson*
Through these prayers, poetry, lyrics, meditations and affirmations, you will share in the strong and undeniable connection women of color share with God.
5 x 7¼, 208 pp, Quality PB, 978-1-59473-077-1 **$15.99**

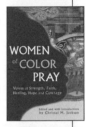

Secrets of Prayer: A Multifaith Guide to Creating Personal Prayer in
Your Life   *by Nancy Corcoran, CSJ*
This compelling, multifaith guidebook offers you companionship and encouragement on the journey to a healthy prayer life. 6 x 9, 160 pp, Quality PB, 978-1-59473-215-7 **$16.99**

Prayers to an Evolutionary God
by William Cleary; Afterword by Diarmuid O'Murchu
Inspired by the spiritual and scientific teachings of Diarmuid O'Murchu and Teilhard de Chardin, reveals that religion and science can be combined to create an expanding view of the universe—an evolutionary faith.
6 x 9, 208 pp, HC, 978-1-59473-006-1 **$21.99**

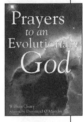

The Art of Public Prayer: Not for Clergy Only   *by Lawrence A. Hoffman*
6 x 9, 288 pp, Quality PB, 978-1-893361-06-5 **$18.99**

A Heart of Stillness: A Complete Guide to Learning the Art of Meditation
by David A. Cooper 5½ x 8½, 272 pp, Quality PB, 978-1-893361-03-4 **$16.95**

Meditation without Gurus: A Guide to the Heart of Practice
by Clark Strand 5½ x 8½, 192 pp, Quality PB, 978-1-893361-93-5 **$16.95**

Praying with Our Hands: 21 Practices of Embodied Prayer from the World's
Spiritual Traditions   *by Jon M. Sweeney; Photographs by Jennifer J. Wilson; Foreword by Mother Tessa
Bielecki; Afterword by Taitetsu Unno, PhD*
8 x 8, 96 pp, 22 duotone photos, Quality PB, 978-1-893361-16-4 **$16.95**

Silence, Simplicity & Solitude: A Complete Guide to Spiritual Retreat at Home
by David A. Cooper 5½ x 8½, 336 pp, Quality PB, 978-1-893361-04-1 **$16.95**

Three Gates to Meditation Practice: A Personal Journey into Sufism, Buddhism,
and Judaism   *by David A. Cooper* 5½ x 8½, 240 pp, Quality PB, 978-1-893361-22-5 **$16.95**

Prayer / M. Basil Pennington, OCSO

Finding Grace at the Center, 3rd Ed.: The Beginning of Centering
Prayer   *with Thomas Keating, OCSO, and Thomas E. Clarke, SJ; Foreword by Rev. Cynthia Bourgeault, PhD*
A practical guide to a simple and beautiful form of meditative prayer.
5 x 7¼, 128 pp, Quality PB, 978-1-59473-182-2 **$12.99**

The Monks of Mount Athos: A Western Monk's Extraordinary
Spiritual Journey on Eastern Holy Ground   *Foreword by Archimandrite Dionysios*
Explores the landscape, the monastic communities, and the food of Athos.
6 x 9, 256 pp, 10+ b/w drawings, Quality PB, 978-1-893361-78-2 **$18.95**

Psalms: A Spiritual Commentary   *Illustrations by Phillip Ratner*
Reflections on some of the most beloved passages from the Bible's most widely read book.   6 x 9, 176 pp, 24 full-page b/w illus., Quality PB, 978-1-59473-234-8 **$16.99**
HC, 978-1-59473-141-9 **$19.99**

The Song of Songs: A Spiritual Commentary   *Illustrations by Phillip Ratner*
Explore the Bible's most challenging mystical text.
6 x 9, 160 pp, 14 b/w illus., Quality PB, 978-1-59473-235-3 **$16.99**; HC, 978-1-59473-004-7 **$19.99**

Midrash Fiction / Folktales

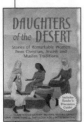

Abraham's Bind & Other Bible Tales of Trickery, Folly, Mercy and Love by Michael J. Caduto

New retellings of episodes in the lives of familiar biblical characters explore relevant life lessons.

6 x 9, 224 pp, HC, 978-1-59473-186-0 **$19.99**

Daughters of the Desert: Stories of Remarkable Women from Christian, Jewish and Muslim Traditions by Claire Rudolf Murphy, Meghan Nuttall Sayres, Mary Cronk Farrell, Sarah Conover and Betsy Wharton

Breathes new life into the old tales of our female ancestors in faith. Uses traditional scriptural passages as starting points, then with vivid detail fills in historical context and place. Chapters reveal the voices of Sarah, Hagar, Huldah, Esther, Salome, Mary Magdalene, Lydia, Khadija, Fatima and many more. Historical fiction ideal for readers of all ages. Quality paperback includes reader's discussion guide.

5½ x 8½, 192 pp, Quality PB, 978-1-59473-106-8 **$14.99**
HC, 192 pp, 978-1-893361-72-0 **$19.95**

The Triumph of Eve & Other Subversive Bible Tales
by Matt Biers-Ariel

Many people were taught and remember only a one-dimensional Bible. These engaging retellings are the antidote to this—they're witty, often hilarious, always profound, and invite you to grapple with questions and issues that are often hidden in the original text.

5½ x 8½, 192 pp, Quality PB, 978-1-59473-176-1 **$14.99**

Also avail.: **The Triumph of Eve Teacher's Guide**
8½ x 11, 44 pp, PB, 978-1-59473-152-5 **$8.99**

Wisdom in the Telling
Finding Inspiration and Grace in Traditional Folktales and Myths Retold
by Lorraine Hartin-Gelardi
6 x 9, 224 pp, HC, 978-1-59473-185-3 **$19.99**

Religious Etiquette / Reference

How to Be a Perfect Stranger, 4th Edition: The Essential Religious Etiquette Handbook Edited by Stuart M. Matlins and Arthur J. Magida

The indispensable guidebook to help the well-meaning guest when visiting other people's religious ceremonies. A straightforward guide to the rituals and celebrations of the major religions and denominations in the United States and Canada from the perspective of an interested guest of any other faith, based on information obtained from authorities of each religion. Belongs in every living room, library and office. Covers:

African American Methodist Churches • Assemblies of God • Bahá'í • Baptist • Buddhist • Christian Church (Disciples of Christ) • Christian Science (Church of Christ, Scientist) • Churches of Christ • Episcopalian and Anglican • Hindu • Islam • Jehovah's Witnesses • Jewish • Lutheran • Mennonite/Amish • Methodist • Mormon (Church of Jesus Christ of Latter-day Saints) • Native American/First Nations • Orthodox Churches • Pentecostal Church of God • Presbyterian • Quaker (Religious Society of Friends) • Reformed Church in America/Canada • Roman Catholic • Seventh-day Adventist • Sikh • Unitarian Universalist • United Church of Canada • United Church of Christ

6 x 9, 432 pp, Quality PB, 978-1-59473-140-2 **$19.99**

The Perfect Stranger's Guide to Funerals and Grieving Practices: A Guide to Etiquette in Other People's Religious Ceremonies Edited by Stuart M. Matlins
6 x 9, 240 pp, Quality PB, 978-1-893361-20-1 **$16.95**

The Perfect Stranger's Guide to Wedding Ceremonies: A Guide to Etiquette in Other People's Religious Ceremonies Edited by Stuart M. Matlins
6 x 9, 208 pp, Quality PB, 978-1-893361-19-5 **$16.95**

Sacred Texts—SkyLight Illuminations Series

Offers today's spiritual seeker an accessible entry into the great classic texts of the world's spiritual traditions. Each classic is presented in an accessible translation, with facing pages of guided commentary from experts, giving you the keys you need to understand the history, context and meaning of the text. This series enables you, whatever your background, to experience and understand classic spiritual texts directly, and to make them a part of your life.

CHRISTIANITY

The End of Days: Essential Selections from Apocalyptic Texts—
Annotated & Explained *Annotation by Robert G. Clouse*
Helps you understand the complex Christian visions of the end of the world.
5½ x 8½, 224 pp, Quality PB, 978-1-59473-170-9 **$16.99**

The Hidden Gospel of Matthew: Annotated & Explained
Translation & Annotation by Ron Miller
Takes you deep into the text cherished around the world to discover the words and events that have the strongest connection to the historical Jesus.
5½ x 8½, 272 pp, Quality PB, 978-1-59473-038-2 **$16.99**

The Lost Sayings of Jesus: Teachings from Ancient Christian, Jewish,
Gnostic and Islamic Sources—Annotated & Explained
Translation & Annotation by Andrew Phillip Smith; Foreword by Stephan A. Hoeller
This collection of more than three hundred sayings depicts Jesus as a Wisdom teacher who speaks to people of all faiths as a mystic and spiritual master.
5½ x 8½, 240 pp, Quality PB, 978-1-59473-172-3 **$16.99**

Philokalia: The Eastern Christian Spiritual Texts—Selections Annotated &
Explained *Annotation by Allyne Smith; Translation by G. E. H. Palmer, Phillip Sherrard and Bishop Kallistos Ware*
The first approachable introduction to the wisdom of the Philokalia, which is the classic text of Eastern Christian spirituality.
5½ x 8½, 240 pp, Quality PB, 978-1-59473-103-7 **$16.99**

The Sacred Writings of Paul: Selections Annotated & Explained
Translation & Annotation by Ron Miller
Explores the apostle Paul's core message of spiritual equality, freedom and joy.
5½ x 8½, 224 pp, Quality PB, 978-1-59473-213-3 **$16.99**

Sex Texts from the Bible: Selections Annotated & Explained
Translation & Annotation by Teresa J. Hornsby; Foreword by Amy-Jill Levine
Offers surprising insight into our modern sexual lives.
5½ x 8½, 208 pp, Quality PB, 978-1-59473-217-1 **$16.99**

Spiritual Writings on Mary: Annotated & Explained
Annotation by Mary Ford-Grabowsky; Foreword by Andrew Harvey
Examines the role of Mary, the mother of Jesus, as a source of inspiration in history and in life today. 5½ x 8½, 288 pp, Quality PB, 978-1-59473-001-6 **$16.99**

The Way of a Pilgrim: The Jesus Prayer Journey—Annotated & Explained
Translation & Annotation by Gleb Pokrovsky; Foreword by Andrew Harvey
This classic of Russian spirituality is the delightful account of one man who sets out to learn the prayer of the heart, also known as the "Jesus prayer."
5½ x 8½, 160 pp, Illus., Quality PB, 978-1-893361-31-7 **$14.95**

Sacred Texts—cont.

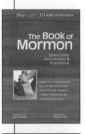

MORMONISM

The Book of Mormon: Selections Annotated & Explained
Annotation by Jana Riess; Foreword by Phyllis Tickle
Explores the sacred epic that is cherished by more than twelve million members of the LDS church as the keystone of their faith.
5½ x 8½ , 272 pp, Quality PB, 978-1-59473-076-4 **$16.99**

NATIVE AMERICAN

Native American Stories of the Sacred: Annotated & Explained
Retold & Annotated by Evan T. Pritchard
Intended for more than entertainment, these teaching tales contain elegantly simple illustrations of time-honored truths.
5½ x 8½, 272 pp, Quality PB, 978-1-59473-112-9 **$16.99**

GNOSTICISM

Gnostic Writings on the Soul: Annotated & Explained
Translation & Annotation by Andrew Phillip Smith; Foreword by Stephan A. Hoeller
Reveals the inspiring ways your soul can remember and return to its unique, divine purpose.
5½ x 8½, 144 pp, Quality PB, 978-1-59473-220-1 **$16.99**

The Gospel of Philip: Annotated & Explained
Translation & Annotation by Andrew Phillip Smith; Foreword by Stevan Davies
Reveals otherwise unrecorded sayings of Jesus and fragments of Gnostic mythology.
5½ x 8½, 160 pp, Quality PB, 978-1-59473-111-2 **$16.99**

The Gospel of Thomas: Annotated & Explained
Translation & Annotation by Stevan Davies Sheds new light on the origins of Christianity and portrays Jesus as a wisdom-loving sage.
5½ x 8½, 192 pp, Quality PB, 978-1-893361-45-4 **$16.99**

The Secret Book of John: The Gnostic Gospel—Annotated & Explained
Translation & Annotation by Stevan Davies The most significant and influential text of the ancient Gnostic religion.
5½ x 8½, 208 pp, Quality PB, 978-1-59473-082-5 **$16.99**

JUDAISM

The Divine Feminine in Biblical Wisdom Literature
Selections Annotated & Explained
Translation & Annotation by Rabbi Rami Shapiro; Foreword by Rev. Cynthia Bourgeault, PhD
Uses the Hebrew books of Psalms, Proverbs, Song of Songs, Ecclesiastes and Job, Wisdom literature and the Wisdom of Solomon to clarify who Wisdom is.
5½ x 8½, 240 pp, Quality PB, 978-1-59473-109-9 **$16.99**

Ethics of the Sages: *Pirke Avot*—Annotated & Explained
Translation & Annotation by Rabbi Rami Shapiro Clarifies the ethical teachings of the early Rabbis. 5½ x 8½, 192 pp, Quality PB, 978-1-59473-207-2 **$16.99**

Hasidic Tales: Annotated & Explained
Translation & Annotation by Rabbi Rami Shapiro
Introduces the legendary tales of the impassioned Hasidic rabbis, presenting them as stories rather than as parables. 5½ x 8½, 240 pp, Quality PB, 978-1-893361-86-7 **$16.95**

The Hebrew Prophets: Selections Annotated & Explained
Translation & Annotation by Rabbi Rami Shapiro; Foreword by Zalman M. Schachter-Shalomi
Focuses on the central themes covered by all the Hebrew prophets.
5½ x 8½, 224 pp, Quality PB, 978-1-59473-037-5 **$16.99**

Zohar: Annotated & Explained *Translation & Annotation by Daniel C. Matt*
The best-selling author of *The Essential Kabbalah* brings together in one place the most important teachings of the Zohar, the canonical text of Jewish mystical tradition.
5½ x 8½, 176 pp, Quality PB, 978-1-893361-51-5 **$15.99**

Sacred Texts—cont.

ISLAM

The Qur'an and Sayings of Prophet Muhammad
Selections Annotated & Explained
Annotation by Sohaib N. Sultan; Translation by Yusuf Ali; Revised by Sohaib N. Sultan
Foreword by Jane I. Smith
Explores how the timeless wisdom of the Qur'an can enrich your own spiritual journey.
5½ x 8½, 256 pp, Quality PB, 978-1-59473-222-5 **$16.99**

Rumi and Islam: Selections from His Stories, Poems, and Discourses—Annotated & Explained
Translation & Annotation by Ibrahim Gamard
Focuses on Rumi's place within the Sufi tradition of Islam, providing insight into the mystical side of the religion.
5½ x 8½, 240 pp, Quality PB, 978-1-59473-002-3 **$15.99**

EASTERN RELIGIONS

The Art of War—Spirituality for Conflict
Annotated & Explained
by Sun Tzu; Annotation by Thomas Huynh; Translation by Thomas Huynh and the Editors at Sonshi.com; Foreword by Thomas Cleary; Preface by Marc Benioff
Highlights principles that encourage a perceptive and spiritual approach to conflict.
5½ x 8½, 192 pp (est), Quality PB, 978-1-59473-244-7 **$16.99**

Bhagavad Gita: Annotated & Explained
Translation by Shri Purohit Swami; Annotation by Kendra Crossen Burroughs
Explains references and philosophical terms, shares the interpretations of famous spiritual leaders and scholars, and more.
5½ x 8½, 192 pp, Quality PB, 978-1-893361-28-7 **$16.95**

Dhammapada: Annotated & Explained
Translation by Max Müller and revised by Jack Maguire; Annotation by Jack Maguire
Contains all of Buddhism's key teachings.
5½ x 8½, 160 pp, b/w photos, Quality PB, 978-1-893361-42-3 **$14.95**

Selections from the Gospel of Sri Ramakrishna
Annotated & Explained
Translation by Swami Nikhilananda; Annotation by Kendra Crossen Burroughs
Introduces the fascinating world of the Indian mystic and the universal appeal of his message.
5½ x 8½, 240 pp, b/w photos, Quality PB, 978-1-893361-46-1 **$16.95**

Tao Te Ching: Annotated & Explained
Translation & Annotation by Derek Lin; Foreword by Lama Surya Das
Introduces an Eastern classic in an accessible, poetic and completely original way.
5½ x 8½, 192 pp, Quality PB, 978-1-59473-204-1 **$16.99**

STOICISM

The Meditations of Marcus Aurelius
Selections Annotated & Explained
Annotation by Russell McNeil, PhD; Translation by George Long; Revised by Russell McNeil, PhD
Offers insightful and engaging commentary into the historical background of Stoicism.
5½ x 8½, 288 pp, Quality PB, 978-1-59473-236-2 **$16.99**

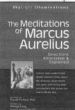

Spirituality of the Seasons

Autumn: A Spiritual Biography of the Season
Edited by Gary Schmidt and Susan M. Felch; Illustrations by Mary Azarian
Rejoice in autumn as a time of preparation and reflection. Includes Wendell Berry, David James Duncan, Robert Frost, A. Bartlett Giamatti, E. B. White, P. D. James, Julian of Norwich, Garret Keizer, Tracy Kidder, Anne Lamott, May Sarton.
6 x 9, 320 pp, 5 b/w illus., Quality PB, 978-1-59473-118-1 **$18.99**

Spring: A Spiritual Biography of the Season
Edited by Gary Schmidt and Susan M. Felch; Illustrations by Mary Azarian
Explore the gentle unfurling of spring and reflect on how nature celebrates rebirth and renewal. Includes Jane Kenyon, Lucy Larcom, Harry Thurston, Nathaniel Hawthorne, Noel Perrin, Annie Dillard, Martha Ballard, Barbara Kingsolver, Dorothy Wordsworth, Donald Hall, David Brill, Lionel Basney, Isak Dinesen, Paul Laurence Dunbar. 6 x 9, 352 pp, 6 b/w illus., Quality PB, 978-1-59473-246-1 **$18.99**

Summer: A Spiritual Biography of the Season
Edited by Gary Schmidt and Susan M. Felch; Illustrations by Barry Moser
"A sumptuous banquet.... These selections lift up an exquisite wholeness found within an everyday sophistication."— H *Publishers Weekly* starred review
Includes Anne Lamott, Luci Shaw, Ray Bradbury, Richard Selzer, Thomas Lynch, Walt Whitman, Carl Sandburg, Sherman Alexie, Madeleine L'Engle, Jamaica Kincaid.
6 x 9, 304 pp, 5 b/w illus., Quality PB, 978-1-59473-183-9 **$18.99**
HC, 978-1-59473-083-2 **$21.99**

Winter: A Spiritual Biography of the Season
Edited by Gary Schmidt and Susan M. Felch; Illustrations by Barry Moser
"This outstanding anthology features top-flight nature and spirituality writers on the fierce, inexorable season of winter.... Remarkably lively and warm, despite the icy subject." — H *Publishers Weekly* starred review
Includes Will Campbell, Rachel Carson, Annie Dillard, Donald Hall, Ron Hansen, Jane Kenyon, Jamaica Kincaid, Barry Lopez, Kathleen Norris, John Updike, E. B. White.
6 x 9, 288 pp, 6 b/w illus., Deluxe PB w/flaps, 978-1-893361-92-8 **$18.95**
HC, 978-1-893361-53-9 **$21.95**

Spirituality / Animal Companions

Blessing the Animals: Prayers and Ceremonies to Celebrate God's Creatures, Wild and Tame *Edited by Lynn L. Caruso* 5 x 7¼, 256 pp, HC, 978-1-59473-145-7 **$19.99**

Remembering My Pet: A Kid's Own Spiritual Workbook for When a Pet Dies
by Nechama Liss-Levinson, PhD, and Rev. Molly Phinney Baskette, MDiv; Foreword by Lynn L. Caruso
8 x 10, 48 pp, 2-color text, HC, 978-1-59473-221-3 **$16.99**

What Animals Can Teach Us about Spirituality: Inspiring Lessons from Wild and Tame Creatures *by Diana L. Guerrero* 6 x 9, 176 pp, Quality PB, 978-1-893361-84-3 **$16.95**

Spirituality—A Week Inside

Come and Sit: A Week Inside Meditation Centers
by Marcia Z. Nelson; Foreword by Wayne Teasdale
6 x 9, 224 pp, b/w photos, Quality PB, 978-1-893361-35-5 **$16.95**

Lighting the Lamp of Wisdom: A Week Inside a Yoga Ashram
by John Ittner; Foreword by Dr. David Frawley
6 x 9, 192 pp, 10+ b/w photos, Quality PB, 978-1-893361-52-2 **$15.95**

Making a Heart for God: A Week Inside a Catholic Monastery
by Dianne Aprile; Foreword by Brother Patrick Hart, ocso
6 x 9, 224 pp, b/w photos, Quality PB, 978-1-893361-49-2 **$16.95**

Waking Up: A Week Inside a Zen Monastery
by Jack Maguire; Foreword by John Daido Loori, Roshi
6 x 9, 224 pp, b/w photos, Quality PB, 978-1-893361-55-3 **$16.95**; HC, 978-1-893361-13-3 **$21.95**

Spirituality

Next to Godliness: Finding the Sacred in Housekeeping
Edited and with Introductions by Alice Peck
Offers new perspectives on how we can reach out for the Divine.
6 x 9, 224 pp, Quality PB, 978-1-59473-214-0 **$19.99**

Bread, Body, Spirit: Finding the Sacred in Food
Edited and with Introductions by Alice Peck
Explores how food feeds our faith. 6 x 9, 224 pp (est), Quality PB, 978-1-59473-242-3 **$19.99**

Renewal in the Wilderness: A Spiritual Guide to Connecting with God in the Natural World *by John Lionberger*
Reveals the power of experiencing God's presence in many variations of the natural world. 6 x 9, 176 pp, b/w photos, Quality PB, 978-1-59473-219-5 **$16.99**

Honoring Motherhood: Prayers, Ceremonies and Blessings
Edited and with Introductions by Lynn L. Caruso
Journey through the seasons of motherhood. 5 x 7¼, 272 pp, HC, 978-1-59473-239-3 **$19.99**

Soul Fire: Accessing Your Creativity *by Rev. Thomas Ryan, CSP*
Learn to cultivate your creative spirit. 6 x 9, 160 pp, Quality PB, 978-1-59473-243-0 **$16.99**

Technology & Spirituality: How the Information Revolution Affects Our Spiritual Lives *by Stephen K. Spyker* 6 x 9, 176 pp, HC, 978-1-59473-218-8 **$19.99**

Money and the Way of Wisdom: Insights from the Book of Proverbs
by Timothy J. Sandoval, PhD 6 x 9, 192 pp (est), Quality PB, 978-1-59473-245-4 **$16.99**

Awakening the Spirit, Inspiring the Soul
30 Stories of Interspiritual Discovery in the Community of Faiths
Edited by Brother Wayne Teasdale and Martha Howard, MD; Foreword by Joan Borysenko, PhD
6 x 9, 224 pp, HC, 978-1-59473-039-9 **$21.99**

Creating a Spiritual Retirement: A Guide to the Unseen Possibilities in Our Lives
by Molly Srode 6 x 9, 208 pp, b/w photos, Quality PB, 978-1-59473-050-4 **$14.99**
HC, 978-1-893361-75-1 **$19.95**

Finding Hope: Cultivating God's Gift of a Hopeful Spirit
by Marcia Ford 8 x 8, 200 pp, Quality PB, 978-1-59473-211-9 **$16.99**

The Geography of Faith: Underground Conversations on Religious, Political and Social Change *by Daniel Berrigan and Robert Coles* 6 x 9, 224 pp, Quality PB, 978-1-893361-40-9 **$16.95**

Jewish Spirituality: A Brief Introduction for Christians *by Lawrence Kushner*
5½ x 8½, 112 pp, Quality PB, 978-1-58023-150-3 **$12.95** *(a Jewish Lights book)*

Journeys of Simplicity: Traveling Light with Thomas Merton, Bashō, Edward Abbey, Annie Dillard & Others *by Philip Harnden* 5 x 7¼, 144 pp, Quality PB, 978-1-59473-181-5 **$12.99** 128 pp, HC, 978-1-893361-76-8 **$16.95**

Keeping Spiritual Balance As We Grow Older: More than 65 Creative Ways to Use Purpose, Prayer, and the Power of Spirit to Build a Meaningful Retirement
by Molly and Bernie Srode 8 x 8, 224 pp, Quality PB, 978-1-59473-042-9 **$16.99**

Spirituality 101: The Indispensable Guide to Keeping—or Finding—Your Spiritual Life on Campus *by Harriet L. Schwartz, with contributions from college students at nearly thirty campuses across the United States* 6 x 9, 272 pp, Quality PB, 978-1-59473-000-9 **$16.99**

Spiritually Incorrect: Finding God in All the *Wrong* Places *by Dan Wakefield; Illus. by Marian DelVecchio* 5½ x 8½, 192 pp, b/w illus., Quality PB, 978-1-59473-137-2 **$15.99**

Spiritual Manifestos: Visions for Renewed Religious Life in America from Young Spiritual Leaders of Many Faiths *Edited by Niles Elliot Goldstein; Preface by Martin E. Marty*
6 x 9, 256 pp, HC, 978-1-893361-09-6 **$21.95**

A Walk with Four Spiritual Guides: Krishna, Buddha, Jesus, and Ramakrishna
by Andrew Harvey 5½ x 8½, 192 pp, 10 b/w photos & illus., Quality PB, 978-1-59473-138-9 **$15.99**

What Matters: Spiritual Nourishment for Head and Heart
by Frederick Franck 5 x 7¼, 128 pp, 50+ b/w illus., HC, 978-1-59473-013-9 **$16.99**

Who Is My God?, 2nd Edition: An Innovative Guide to Finding Your Spiritual Identity
Created by the Editors at SkyLight Paths 6 x 9, 160 pp, Quality PB, 978-1-59473-014-6 **$15.99**

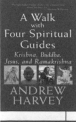

Spiritual Practice

Soul Fire: Accessing Your Creativity *by Rev. Thomas Ryan, CSP*
Shows you how to cultivate your creative spirit as a way to encourage personal growth.
6 x 9, 160 pp, Quality PB, 978-1-59473-243-0 **$16.99**

Running—The Sacred Art: Preparing to Practice
by Dr. Warren A. Kay; Foreword by Kristin Armstrong
Examines how your daily run can enrich your spiritual life.
5½ x 8½, 160 pp, Quality PB, 978-1-59473-227-0 **$16.99**

Hospitality—The Sacred Art: Discovering the Hidden Spiritual Power
of Invitation and Welcome *by Rev. Nanette Sawyer; Foreword by Rev. Dirk Ficca*
Explores how this ancient spiritual practice can transform your relationships.
5½ x 8½, 192 pp, Quality PB, 978-1-59473-228-7 **$16.99**

Thanking & Blessing—The Sacred Art: Spiritual Vitality through
Gratefulness *by Jay Marshall, PhD; Foreword by Philip Gulley*
Offers practical tips for uncovering the blessed wonder in our lives—even in trying circumstances. 5½ x 8½, 176 pp, Quality PB, 978-1-59473-231-7 **$16.99**

Everyday Herbs in Spiritual Life: A Guide to Many Practices
by Michael J. Caduto; Foreword by Rosemary Gladstar Explores the power of herbs.
7 x 9, 208 pp, 21 b/w illustrations, Quality PB, 978-1-59473-174-7 **$16.99**

Divining the Body: Reclaim the Holiness of Your Physical Self *by Jan Phillips*
8 x 8, 256 pp, Quality PB, 978-1-59473-080-1 **$16.99**

Finding Time for the Timeless: Spirituality in the Workweek
by John McQuiston II Simple stories show you how refocus your daily life.
5½ x 6¾, 208 pp, HC, 978-1-59473-035-1 **$17.99**

The Gospel of Thomas: A Guidebook for Spiritual Practice
by Ron Miller; Translations by Stevan Davies
6 x 9, 160 pp, Quality PB, 978-1-59473-047-4 **$14.99**

Earth, Water, Fire, and Air: Essential Ways of Connecting to Spirit
by Cait Johnson 6 x 9, 224 pp, HC, 978-1-893361-65-2 **$19.95**

Labyrinths from the Outside In: Walking to Spiritual Insight—A Beginner's Guide
by Donna Schaper and Carole Ann Camp
6 x 9, 208 pp, b/w illus. and photos, Quality PB, 978-1-893361-18-8 **$16.95**

Practicing the Sacred Art of Listening: A Guide to Enrich Your Relationships
and Kindle Your Spiritual Life—The Listening Center Workshop
by Kay Lindahl 8 x 8, 176 pp, Quality PB, 978-1-893361-85-0 **$16.95**

Releasing the Creative Spirit: Unleash the Creativity in Your Life
by Dan Wakefield 7 x 10, 256 pp, Quality PB, 978-1-893361-36-2 **$16.95**

The Sacred Art of Bowing: Preparing to Practice
by Andi Young 5½ x 8½, 128 pp, b/w illus., Quality PB, 978-1-893361-82-9 **$14.95**

The Sacred Art of Chant: Preparing to Practice
by Ana Hernández 5½ x 8½, 192 pp, Quality PB, 978-1-59473-036-8 **$15.99**

The Sacred Art of Fasting: Preparing to Practice
by Thomas Ryan, CSP 5½ x 8½, 192 pp, Quality PB, 978-1-59473-078-8 **$15.99**

The Sacred Art of Forgiveness: Forgiving Ourselves and Others through God's Grace
by Marcia Ford 8 x 8, 176 pp, Quality PB, 978-1-59473-175-4 **$16.99**

The Sacred Art of Listening: Forty Reflections for Cultivating a Spiritual Practice
by Kay Lindahl; Illustrations by Amy Schnapper
8 x 8, 160 pp, b/w illus., Quality PB, 978-1-893361-44-7 **$16.99**

The Sacred Art of Lovingkindness: Preparing to Practice
by Rabbi Rami Shapiro; Foreword by Marcia Ford 5½ x 8½, 176 pp, Quality PB, 978-1-59473-151-8 **$16.99**

Sacred Speech: A Practical Guide for Keeping Spirit in Your Speech
by Rev. Donna Schaper 6 x 9, 176 pp, Quality PB, 978-1-59473-068-9 **$15.99**
HC, 978-1-893361-74-4 **$21.95**

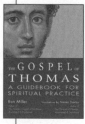

Spirituality & Crafts

The Knitting Way
A Guide to Spiritual Self-Discovery
by Linda Skolnik and Janice MacDaniels
Examines how you can explore and strengthen your spiritual life through knitting.
7 x 9, 240 pp, Quality PB, b/w photographs, 978-1-59473-079-5 **$16.99**

The Scrapbooking Journey
A Hands-On Guide to Spiritual Discovery
by Cory Richardson-Lauve; Foreword by Stacy Julian
Reveals how this craft can become a practice used to deepen and shape your life.
7 x 9, 176 pp, Quality PB, 8-page full-color insert, plus b/w photographs
978-1-59473-216-4 **$18.99**

The Painting Path
Embodying Spiritual Discovery through Yoga, Brush and Color
by Linda Novick; Foreword by Richard Segalman
Explores the divine connection you can experience through creativity.
7 x 9, 208 pp, 8-page full-color insert, plus b/w photographs
Quality PB, 978-1-59473-226-3 **$18.99**

The Quilting Path
A Guide to Spiritual Discovery through Fabric, Thread and Kabbalah
by Louise Silk
Explores how to cultivate personal growth through quilt making.
7 x 9, 192 pp, Quality PB, b/w photographs and illustrations, 978-1-59473-206-5 **$16.99**

Contemplative Crochet
A Hands-On Guide for Interlocking Faith and Craft
by Cindy Crandall-Frazier; Foreword by Linda Skolnik
Illuminates the spiritual lessons you can learn through crocheting.
7 x 9, 192 pp (est), b/w photographs, Quality PB, 978-1-59473-238-6 **$16.99**

Kabbalah / Enneagram
(from Jewish Lights Publishing)

Awakening to Kabbalah: The Guiding Light of Spiritual Fulfillment
by Rav Michael Laitman, PhD 6 x 9, 192 pp, HC, 978-1-58023-264-7 **$21.99**

Cast in God's Image: Discover Your Personality Type Using the Enneagram and Kabbalah
by Rabbi Howard A. Addison 7 x 9, 176 pp, Quality PB, 978-1-58023-124-4 **$16.95**

Ehyeh: A Kabbalah for Tomorrow *by Dr. Arthur Green*
6 x 9, 224 pp, Quality PB, 978-1-58023-213-5 **$16.99**

The Enneagram and Kabbalah, 2nd Edition: Reading Your Soul
by Rabbi Howard A. Addison 6 x 9, 192 pp, Quality PB, 978-1-58023-229-6 **$16.99**

The Gift of Kabbalah: Discovering the Secrets of Heaven, Renewing Your Life on Earth
by Tamar Frankiel, PhD 6 x 9, 256 pp, Quality PB, 978-1-58023-141-1 **$16.95**
HC, 978-1-58023-108-4 **$21.95**

Kabbalah: A Brief Introduction for Christians
by Tamar Frankiel, PhD 5½ x 8½, 176 pp, Quality PB, 978-1-58023-303-3 **$16.99**

Zohar: Annotated & Explained *Translation and Annotation by Dr. Daniel C. Matt*
Foreword by Andrew Harvey 5½ x 8½, 176 pp, Quality PB, 978-1-893361-51-5 **$15.99**
(a SkyLight Paths book)

About SKYLIGHT PATHS Publishing

SkyLight Paths Publishing is creating a place where people of different spiritual traditions come together for challenge and inspiration, a place where we can help each other understand the mystery that lies at the heart of our existence.

Through spirituality, our religious beliefs are increasingly becoming a part of our lives—rather than *apart* from our lives. While many of us may be more interested than ever in spiritual growth, we may be less firmly planted in traditional religion. Yet, we do want to deepen our relationship to the sacred, to learn from our own as well as from other faith traditions, and to practice in new ways.

SkyLight Paths sees both believers and seekers as a community that increasingly transcends traditional boundaries of religion and denomination—people wanting to learn from each other, *walking together, finding the way.*

For your information and convenience, at the back of this book we have provided a list of other SkyLight Paths books you might find interesting and useful. They cover the following subjects:

Buddhism / Zen	Global Spiritual	Monasticism
Catholicism	Perspectives	Mysticism
Children's Books	Gnosticism	Poetry
Christianity	Hinduism /	Prayer
Comparative	Vedanta	Religious Etiquette
Religion	Inspiration	Retirement
Current Events	Islam / Sufism	Spiritual Biography
Earth-Based	Judaism	Spiritual Direction
Spirituality	Kabbalah	Spirituality
Enneagram	Meditation	Women's Interest
	Midrash Fiction	Worship

Or phone, fax, mail or e-mail to: **SKYLIGHT PATHS Publishing**
Sunset Farm Offices, Route 4 • P.O. Box 237 • Woodstock, Vermont 05091
Tel: (802) 457-4000 • Fax: (802) 457-4004 • www.skylightpaths.com
Credit card orders: **(800) 962-4544** (8:30AM–5:30PM ET Monday–Friday)
Generous discounts on quantity orders. SATISFACTION GUARANTEED. Prices subject to change.